Scenes of North American Wildlife

for the Scroll Saw

BY RICK AND KAREN LONGABAUGH

Fox
Chapel Publishing

1970 Broad Street • East Petersburg, PA 17520
www.FoxChapelPublishing.com

© 2005 by Fox Chapel Publishing Company, Inc.

Scenes of North American Wildlife for the Scroll Saw is a compilation of projects featured in *North American Wildlife* by Rick and Karen Longabaugh. The patterns contained herein are copyrighted by The Berry Basket. Readers may make three copies of these patterns for personal use. The patterns themselves, however, are not to be duplicated for resale or distribution under any circumstances. Any such copying is a violation of copyright law.

Bibliographical note
Scenes of North American Wildlife for the Scroll Saw is a revised and expanded republication of *North American Wildlife*, originally published in 1999. This edition of the work includes expanded instructions for getting started along with full-color photos and a full-color gallery of finished projects.

ISBN–13: 978–1–56523–277–8
ISBN–10: 1–56523–277–1

Publisher's Cataloging-in-Publication Data

Longabaugh, Rick.

    Scenes of North American wildlife for the scroll saw / by Rick and Karen Longabaugh. -- East Petersburg, PA : Fox Chapel Publishing, c2005.

        p. ; cm.

    Includes index.
    ISBN: 1-56523-277-1
    ISBN-13: 978-1-56523-277-8

    1. Wood-carving--Technique. 2. Wood-carving--Patterns.
    3. Wildlife wood-carving--Patterns. I. Longabaugh, Karen. II. Title.

TT199.7 .L666 2005
736/.4--dc22   0509

Printed in China
10 9 8 7 6 5 4 3 2 1

Alan Giagnocavo
Publisher

Peg Couch
Acquisition Editor

Gretchen Bacon
Editor

Troy Thorne
Design

Linda L. Eberly
Jon Deck
Layout

Jon Deck
Cover Design

To learn more about the other great books from Fox Chapel Publishing, or to find a retailer near you, call toll-free 1-800-457-9112 or visit us at **www.FoxChapelPublishing.com**.

Note to Authors: we are always looking for talented authors to write new books in our area of woodworking, design, and related crafts. Please send a brief letter describing your idea to Peg Couch, Acquisition Editor, 1970 Broad Street, East Petersburg, PA 17520.

TABLE OF CONTENTS

Rick and Karen Longabaugh started The Berry Basket and Great American Scrollsaw Patterns—their family-owned online and mail order company, specializing in unique and useful scroll saw patterns and accessories—in the fall of 1990. What began as one set of collapsible basket patterns became a complete line of full-size woodworking patterns and hard-to-find accessories.

Rick has been featured on the popular PBS show *The American Woodshop* with Scott Phillips and also on the cover of *Popular Woodworking* magazine. Many of their unique projects have been published in a number of woodworking publications, including *Wood* magazine, *Creative Woodworks & Crafts*, *Popular Woodworking*, *The Art of the Scroll Saw*, *Scroll Saw Workshop*, and Patrick Spielman's *Home Workshop News*.

INTRODUCTION

T he 3-D layer technique has proven to be a very popular form of scroll saw art. Veining, along with spacers of different thicknesses behind the figures, gives this unique form of scroll sawing its realistic appearance.

This book features a wide variety of projects from The Berry Basket's unique collection of wildlife scenes. These fantastic projects are great for gifts as well as for earning extra income. Precise patterns and easy-to-follow instructions will enable you to complete your project with professional results, and you'll also find some basic scroll sawing tips and techniques to get you started.

The natural beauty captured in each and every one of the designs will simply take your breath away. But please be forewarned: these projects are destined to become treasured family heirlooms for generations to come. You may find yourself having to make more than one for each member of your family!

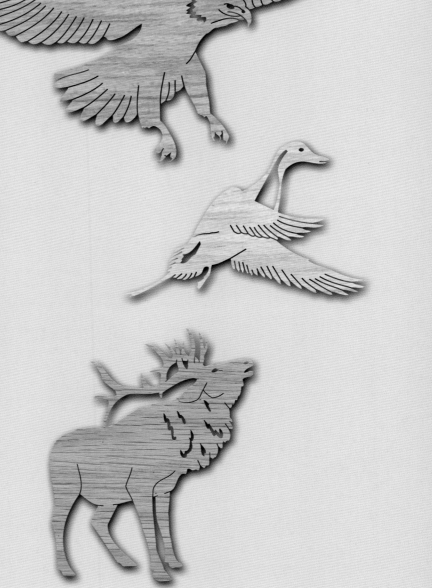

GETTING STARTED

The following scroll saw tips and techniques are intended to get you started and on your way to scroll saw success. You will find these techniques helpful in completing the projects in this book as well as other scroll saw projects.

SAFETY TIPS

Always keep safety in mind as you are working. Here are some general safety guidelines to take into consideration before you begin.

Figure 1. Be sure to sand the workpiece before applying the pattern. You may also want to sand the wood lightly once you have cut the design and removed the pattern to eliminate any "fuzz" and to get rid of any glue residue.

• Use glasses, goggles, or similar equipment to protect your eyes.
• Remove any loose clothing or jewelry before you operate your saw.
• It is always a good idea to work in a well-ventilated area. Consider using a mask, an air cleaner, a dust collector, or any combination of these to protect your lungs from fine dust.
• Be sure that your work area is well lighted.
• Keep your hands a safe distance away from the blade.
• Don't work when you are tired or unfocused.

COPYING THE PATTERN

The patterns contained in this book are intended to be your master patterns. We recommend making photocopies of the project pieces and then using a repositionable spray adhesive to adhere them to your workpiece. This method of transfer is easier, less time-consuming, and far more accurate than tracing. Using a photocopier will also allow you to enlarge or reduce the pattern to fit the size of wood you choose to use. Please note that some photocopy machines may cause a slight distortion in size, so it is important to use the same photocopier for all of the pieces of your project and to photocopy your patterns in the same direction. Distortion is more likely to occur on very large patterns.

PREPARING THE SURFACE

For most projects, it is best to sand the workpiece prior to applying the paper pattern and cutting the design (see **Figure 1**). Once you've cut the design

FREE Pattern Offer!

YES! Please sign me up to receive a FREE scroll saw and/or woodcarving pattern.

(Check your choice of pattern at right) ☐ **Woodcarving** ☐ **Scroll Saw**

Previously purchased titles: _____

I'm particularly interested in: (circle all that apply)

| General Woodworking | Woodcarving | Scroll Sawing | Cabinetmaking | Nature Drawing |

Suggestion box:
I think Fox Chapel should do a book about: _____

BONUS *Provide your email address to receive more free patterns and updates!*

Send to:

Name: _____

Address: _____

City: _____ Email Address: _____

State/Prov.: _____

Country: _____ Zip: _____

Please
Place
Postage
Here

From: _____

City: _____
State/Prov.: _____ Zip: _____
Country: _____

Fox Chapel Publishing

Free Pattern Offer
1970 Broad St.
East Petersburg PA 17520   USA

and removed the paper pattern, it may be necessary to lightly sand any glue residue remaining, along with any "fuzz" on the bottom side.

TRANSFERRING THE PATTERN

Using a repositionable spray adhesive is the easiest and quickest way to transfer a pattern to your workpiece after photocopying it. (These adhesives can be found at most arts and crafts, photography, and department stores. Pay special attention to purchase one that states "temporary bond" or "repositionable.")

Start by setting up in a well-ventilated area. Lightly spray the back side of the paper pattern, not the wood (see **Figure 2**). Allow it to dry only until tacky—approximately 20 to 30 seconds. Then, apply it to the workpiece, smoothing any wrinkles if necessary.

One of the most common problems with using repositionable spray adhesive for the first time is applying the right amount onto the back of the pattern. Spraying too little may result in the pattern's lifting off the project while you are cutting. If this occurs, clear Scotch tape or 2" clear packaging tape can be used to secure the pattern back into position. Spraying too much will make it difficult to remove the pattern. If this occurs, simply use a handheld hair dryer to heat the glue, which will loosen the pattern and allow it to be easily removed.

SELECTING THE MATERIALS

Selecting the type of material that you will use is very important for the final outcome of your project. All of the projects in this book have been designed so that hardwoods, plywoods, or a combination can be used to create your work of art.

Hardwoods offer a wide variety of species, colors, and grain patterns; however, they are more time-consuming to cut, require more sanding, are more likely to warp, and are more expensive to use (see **Figure 3**). Generally, any of the domestic or imported varieties will work well—ash, maple, walnut, oak, birch, mahogany, cherry, and hickory are just a few of the common types.

Plywoods, on the other hand, are less expensive, require less sanding, and come in a variety of standard thicknesses. They also are less likely to develop cracks or to warp. We do, however, recommend that you use top-grade plywood without voids, such as the Baltic and Finnish birches.

Figure 2. Use "repositionable" spray adhesive to adhere your patterns to the wood. A simple glue box, made from a common cardboard box, helps to confine the adhesive.

Figure 3. Hardwoods offer a variety of colors and grain patterns that can enhance your projects. Shown here from left to right are catalpa, red oak, cherry, birch, black walnut, white oak, mahogany, and American aromatic cedar.

Skip Tooth Blades

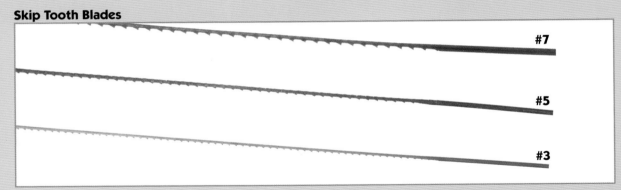

#7

#5

#3

Figure 4. Skip tooth blades can be good blades for a beginning scroller. Pictured here from bottom to top are skip tooth blades #3, #5, and #7.

BLADE SELECTION

There are many opinions regarding which blade to use, depending on which type and thickness of material you choose and on how intricate the design in the project is. The more time you put into scrolling, the more your choice of which blade to use will become personal preference.

For the beginning scroller, we recommend skip tooth blades, but be sure to experiment and find the blade that suits you best (see **Figure 4**). We also offer the following blade size guidelines to get you started:

Material Thickness	Blade Size Recommended
¹⁄₁₆" to ¼"	#2/0, #2, or #3
¼" to ½"	#5 or #7
½" to ¾" or thicker	#7 or #9

SQUARING THE BLADE

Before you begin cutting, it's a good idea to check that your table is square to the blade. Lift the saw arm up to its highest point and place a 2" triangle or a small square beside the blade (see **Figure 5**). If the blade and the square aren't parallel to each other, adjust your table until both the blade and the square line up.

If you don't have a square or triangle, try this method using a piece of scrap wood. First, make a small cut in a piece of scrap wood (see **Figure 6**). Then, turn the scrap wood until the cut is facing the back of the blade. Slide the wood across the table so that the blade fits into the cut. If the blade inserts easily into the cut, it is square. If the blade does not insert easily into the cut, adjust the table until the blade is square.

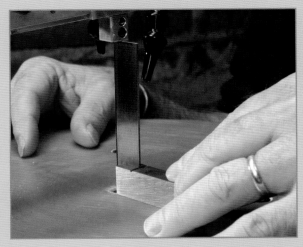

Figure 5. One way to check if your table is square to your blade is to use a small square. Place the square next to the blade and adjust the table as necessary until the blade and the square are parallel.

Figure 6. If you don't have a square, you can use a piece of scrap wood to square the table to the blade. First, make a small cut in the piece of scrap wood. Then, slide the cut toward the blade from the back. If the blade fits into the cut easily, the table is square to the blade.

Figure 7. Drill any blade entry holes after adhering the pattern to the wood. Locate the blade entry holes close to corners so that it will take less time for the blade to reach the pattern line.

CREATING AN AUXILIARY TABLE

Most scroll saws on the market today have an opening in the table and around the blade that is much larger than what you need. This design often causes small and delicate fretwork to break off on the downward stroke of the blade. An easy solution is to add a wooden auxiliary table to the top of the metal table on your saw.

To make an auxiliary table, choose a piece of ¼" to ⅜" plywood that is similar to the size of your current saw's table. If you wish, you can cut this plywood to the same shape as the metal table on your saw, or to any shape or size you prefer. We do recommend, however, that you make the table larger than what you think you will need for the size of the projects you will make in the future.

Next, set the auxiliary table on top of the metal table. From the underside of the metal table, use a pencil to mark the location where the blade will feed through. Then, turn the auxiliary table over and drill a ¹⁄₁₆"- to ⅛"-diameter hole, or a hole slightly larger than the blade you will be using.

Finally, apply a few strips of double-sided carpet tape to the metal table on each side of the blade. Firmly press the auxiliary table onto the double-sided carpet tape, making sure that the blade is centered in the hole.

DRILLING BLADE ENTRY HOLES

If your project requires blade entry holes, be sure to drill all of them once you have adhered the paper pattern to the workpiece with repositionable spray adhesive. When drilling blade entry holes, it is best to drill close to a corner, rather than in the middle of the waste areas, because it will take less time for the blade to reach the pattern line (see **Figure 7**). Sand the back of the piece to remove any burrs before you begin cutting.

VEINING

Veining is a simple technique that will bring a lifelike appearance to your project. The veins of a leaf or the folds of clothing will look more realistic when this technique is incorporated.

To vein, simply choose a thin blade (usually smaller than #7) and saw all solid, black lines as indicated on the pattern. You will be able to vein some areas of the pattern by sawing inward from the outside edge (see **Figure 8**); in other areas, you will need to drill a tiny blade entry hole for the blade.

If you wish to make a project easier, simply omit the veining.

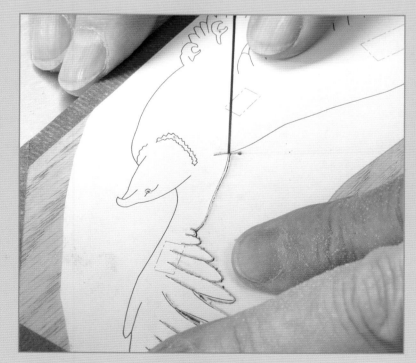

Figure 8. Veining can give your projects a lifelike appearance. Many times veining areas will be as simple as cutting inward from the outside edge.

STACK CUTTING

Stack cutting is fairly simple to do and can save you a lot of time when you have two or more identical pieces to cut for a project or if you are making more than one of a particular project. If you are fairly new to scroll sawing and stack cutting, we recommend cutting no more than a total thickness of ½" for best results.

On projects with fairly simple shapes, two or three layers could be held together by double-sided tape or by paper sprayed on both sides with glue and sandwiched between the workpieces (see **Figure 9**). You could also put masking tape on each edge of the stack to hold the pattern and the workpieces in place.

On more intricate projects, we suggest using #18 wire nails or brads that are slightly longer than the total thickness of the stack you are cutting. Tack the nails into the waste areas you will cut out, along with a few around the outside of the project. If the nail has gone through the bottom of the workpiece, use a hammer to tap it flush or use

coarse sandpaper to sand the points flush with the bottom of the workpiece.

If you are stack cutting hardwoods, do not tack the nail too close to the pattern line or it may cause the wood to split. You could also predrill holes for the nails with a slightly smaller drill bit so the nail will fit snugly and hold the layers together securely.

SAWING THIN WOODS

Thin hardwoods or plywoods can be difficult to work with because they're prone to breaking. The following suggestions should help to eliminate or reduce this problem.

- If you have a variable speed saw, reduce the speed to ½ to ¾ of high speed.
- If you do not have a variable speed saw, it will help to stack cut two or more layers of material to prevent breakage.
- For cutting any thickness of material, it is very beneficial to keep the fingers of at least one hand, if not both, partially touching the table for better control (see **Figure 10**).
- Using a smaller blade with more teeth per inch helps to slow down the speed at which the blade is cutting. However, if the blade is leaving burn marks, you will need to slow the saw speed down or use a blade with fewer teeth per inch.

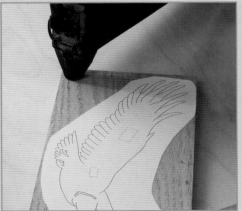

Figure 9. Masking tape or painter's tape (shown) placed around the edges can be used to hold a stack together. Some scrollers also like to cover the surface of the wood with tape before adhering the pattern to help lubricate the blade as it cuts. Driving nails in the corners of the stack can also be an effective method of holding the stack together.

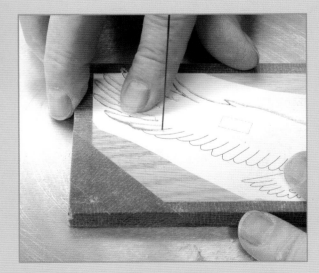

Figure 10. Keeping some of the fingers of both hands in contact with the surface can give you better control.

FINISHING TECHNIQUES

The finishing of 3-D layer projects can be done before or after assembling. If you finish the piece before assembling, you have more options for using contrasting stains.

If you've made your project from hardwood, we recommend dipping it in a dishpan or a similar container filled with a penetrating oil, such as Watco or tung (see **Figure 11**). After dipping the project, allow the excess oil to drain back into the pan, and then follow the manufacturer's instructions.

If you have chosen to use plywood, such as Baltic birch, we recommend using two slightly different shades of stain in order to give an appealing contrast to the finished project.

As a final finish step, use a clear, Varathane-type spray for a protective coating.

ASSEMBLY

Assemble your project by first attaching the six spacer blocks to the back of the frame with glue, cyanoacrylate, or silicone (see **Figure 12**). Center the frame over the back and glue the spacer blocks into position on the back. Attach the spacers where indicated on the back of the figures. Position the figures approximately as shown in the diagram and secure into place (see **Figure 13**).

Note: If you are attaching a banner to the frame, we recommend gluing contrasting paper behind the lettering before gluing the banner in place.

Figure 11. If you have used hardwood for your project, an easy method of finishing is to dip it in a dishpan or a similar container filled with a penetrating oil.

Figure 12. When you are ready to assemble your project, begin by attaching the six spacer blocks to the back of the frame.

CUSTOMIZING YOUR PROJECT

There are several options available to help you customize your scenic 3-D layer project. If you have chosen plywood for parts of your project, veneers are an excellent way to add contrast. When gluing veneers to your workpieces, it is important to glue the veneer to both sides of your material. This will help to prevent the plywood from warping or cupping.

All of the frames and figures in this book are designed to be interchangeable with each other. This will allow you to be creative and to customize your own scenic wilderness masterpiece.

You can also enlarge or reduce the size of the projects. Try making one project at full-size and then a few projects at 50% to 75% for a striking display. Remember to enlarge or reduce the frame, back, and figures by the same percentages. You'll also want to change the thickness of your material in relation to the enlargement or reduction of the piece. For example, if you make a piece that is twice as large, you'll need material that is twice as thick.

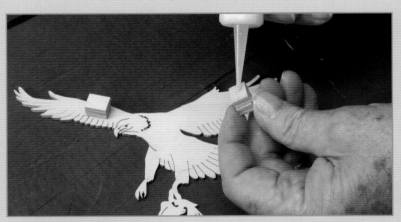

Figure 13. Position the spacers on the backs of the pieces as indicated on the patterns; then, glue the pieces in place using the diagrams provided.

Elk Call, pattern on page 59.

Deer Portrait, pattern on page 43.

Another Day in Paradise, pattern on page 19.

God's Country, pattern on page 35.

On the Wing, pattern on page 87.

Duck in Flight, pattern on page 99.

LAND OF THE FREE

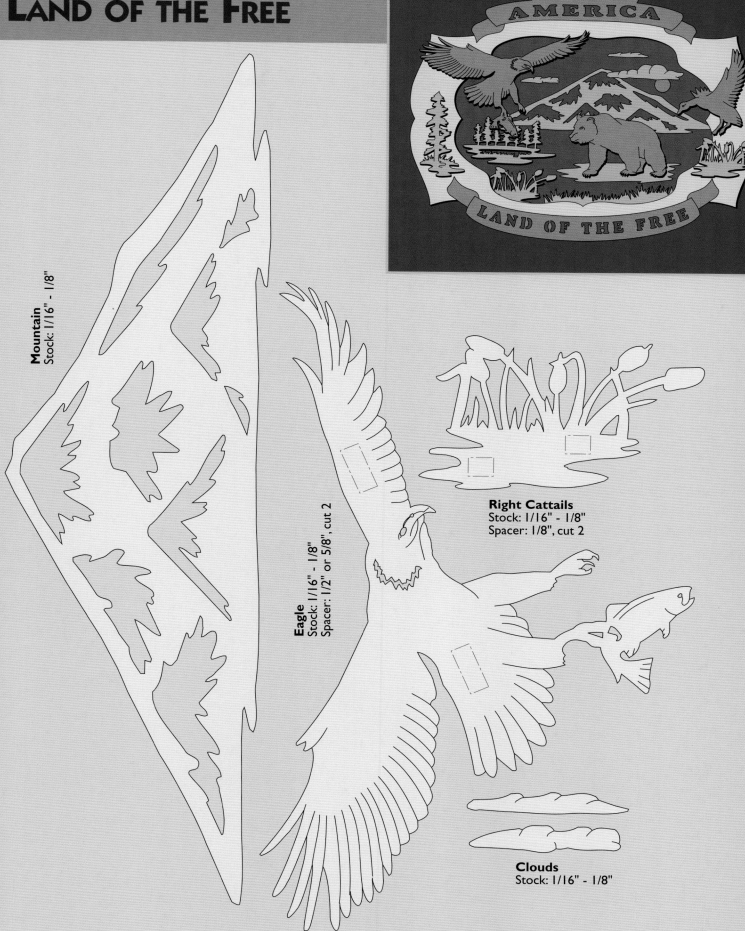

NORTH AMERICA

LAND OF THE FREE

Mountain
Stock: 1/16" - 1/8"

Eagle
Stock: 1/16" - 1/8"
Spacer: 1/2" or 5/8", cut 2

Right Cattails
Stock: 1/16" - 1/8"
Spacer: 1/8", cut 2

Clouds
Stock: 1/16" - 1/8"

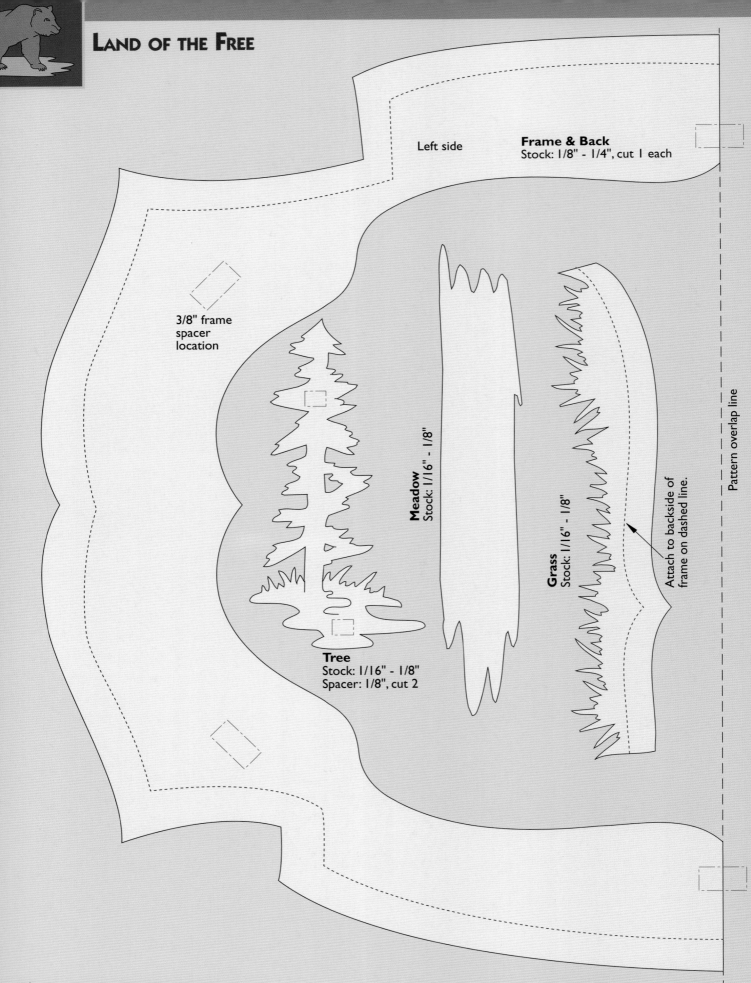

LAND OF THE FREE

Left side

Frame & Back
Stock: 1/8" - 1/4", cut 1 each

3/8" frame spacer location

Tree
Stock: 1/16" - 1/8"
Spacer: 1/8", cut 2

Meadow
Stock: 1/16" - 1/8"

Grass
Stock: 1/16" - 1/8"

Attach to backside of frame on dashed line.

Pattern overlap line

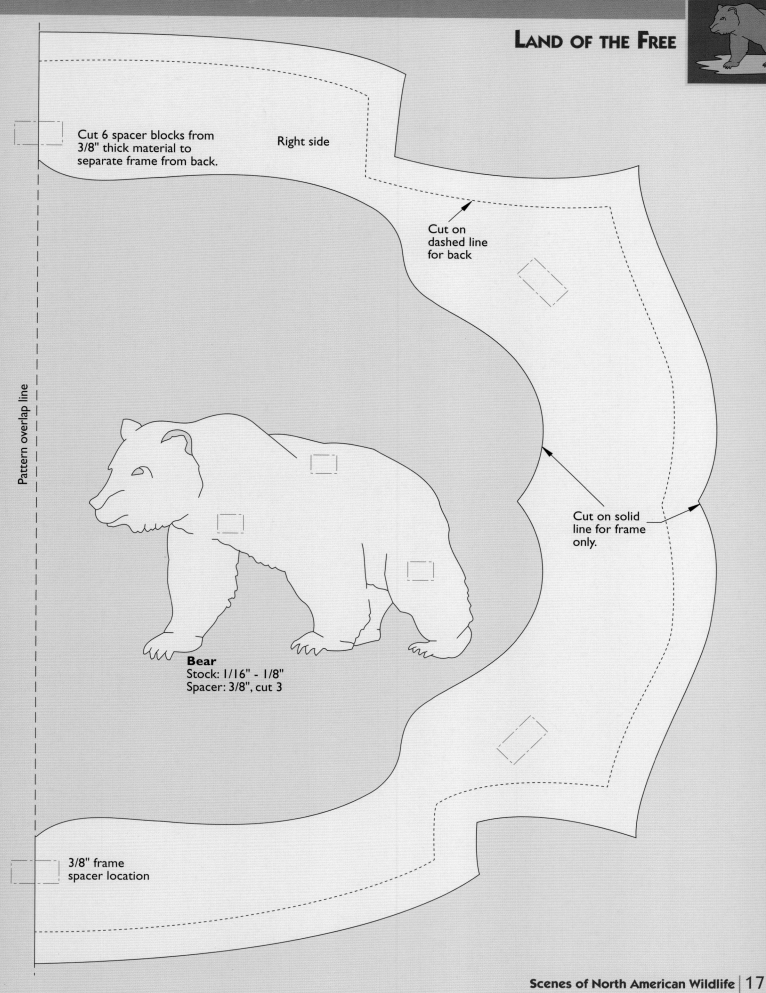

Cut 6 spacer blocks from 3/8" thick material to separate frame from back.

Right side

Cut on dashed line for back

Pattern overlap line

Cut on solid line for frame only.

Bear
Stock: 1/16" - 1/8"
Spacer: 3/8", cut 3

3/8" frame spacer location

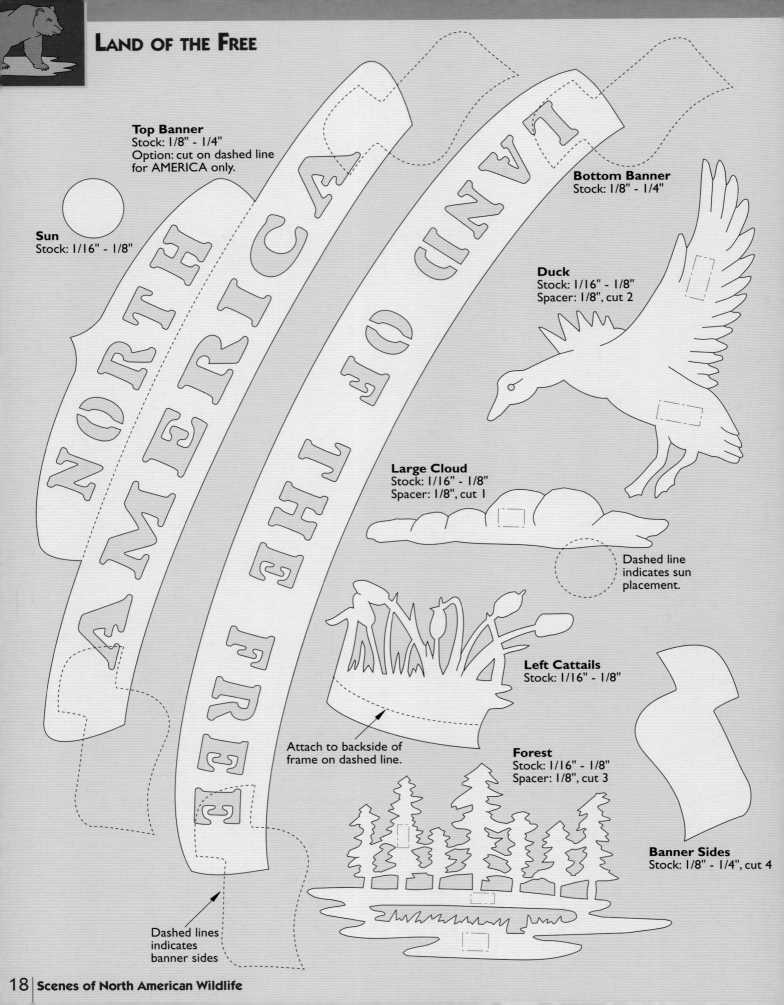

LAND OF THE FREE

Top Banner
Stock: 1/8" - 1/4"
Option: cut on dashed line
for AMERICA only.

Sun
Stock: 1/16" - 1/8"

Bottom Banner
Stock: 1/8" - 1/4"

Duck
Stock: 1/16" - 1/8"
Spacer: 1/8", cut 2

Large Cloud
Stock: 1/16" - 1/8"
Spacer: 1/8", cut 1

Dashed line
indicates sun
placement.

Left Cattails
Stock: 1/16" - 1/8"

Attach to backside of
frame on dashed line.

Forest
Stock: 1/16" - 1/8"
Spacer: 1/8", cut 3

Banner Sides
Stock: 1/8" - 1/4", cut 4

Dashed lines
indicates
banner sides

ANOTHER DAY IN PARADISE

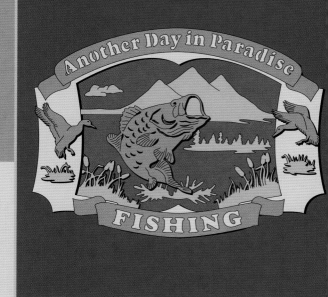

Right Grass
Stock: 1/16" - 1/8"
Spacer: 1/8", cut 1

Mountain
Stock: 1/16" - 1/8"

Right Duck
Stock: 1/16" - 1/8"
Spacer: 1/8", cut 2

Fish
Stock: 1/16" - 1/8"
Spacer: 3/8", cut 3

Forest
Stock: 1/16" - 1/8"
Spacer: 1/8", cut 2

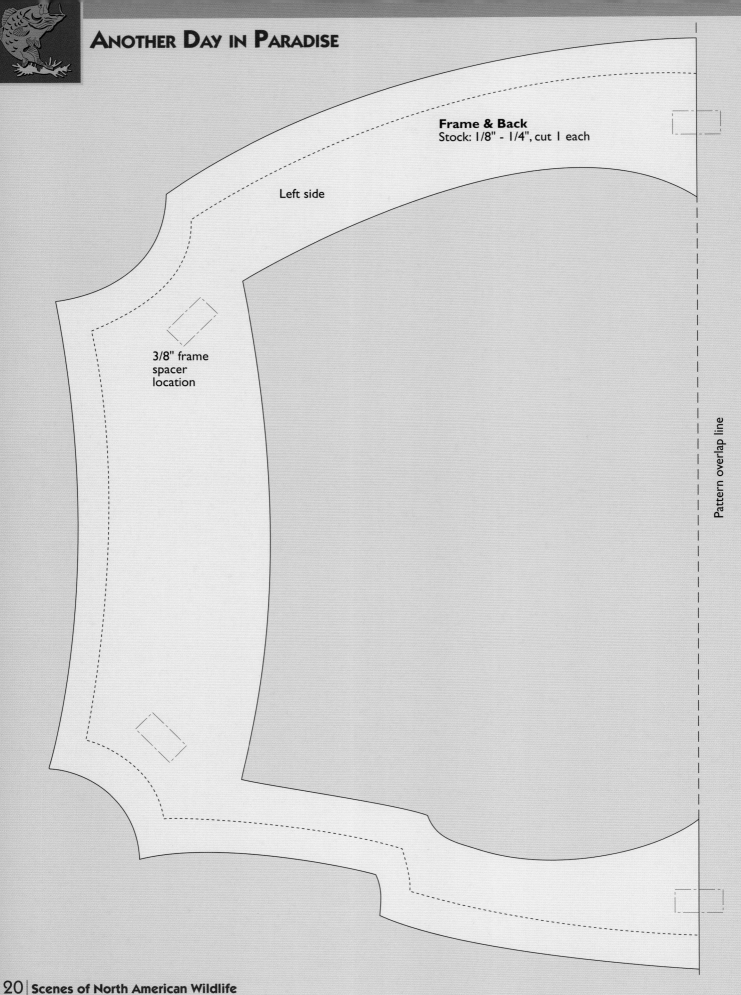

ANOTHER DAY IN PARADISE

Frame & Back
Stock: 1/8" - 1/4", cut 1 each

Left side

3/8" frame
spacer
location

Pattern overlap line

Cut 6 spacer blocks from 3/8" thick material to separate frame from back.

Right side

Cut on dashed line for back

Cut on solid line for frame only.

Right Cattails
Stock: 1/16" - 1/8"

Attach to backside of the frame on dashed line.

Pattern overlap line

3/8" frame spacer location

3/8" frame spacer location

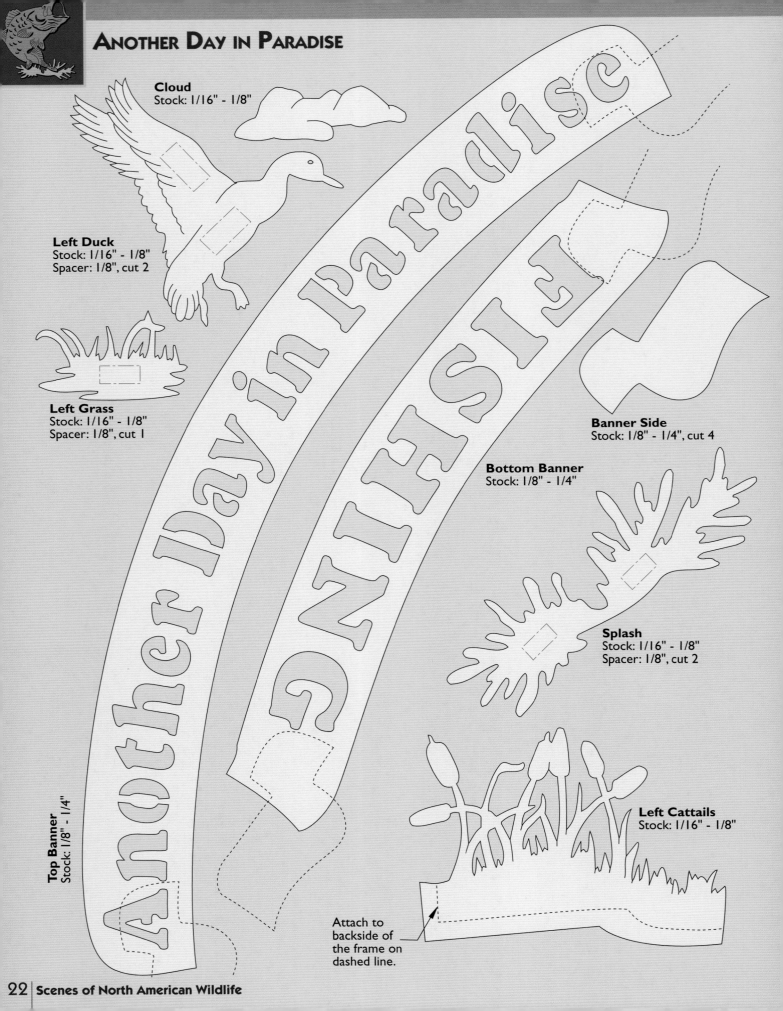

Cloud
Stock: 1/16" - 1/8"

Left Duck
Stock: 1/16" - 1/8"
Spacer: 1/8", cut 2

Left Grass
Stock: 1/16" - 1/8"
Spacer: 1/8", cut 1

Top Banner
Stock: 1/8" - 1/4"

Another Day in Paradise

FISHING

Banner Side
Stock: 1/8" - 1/4", cut 4

Bottom Banner
Stock: 1/8" - 1/4"

Splash
Stock: 1/16" - 1/8"
Spacer: 1/8", cut 2

Left Cattails
Stock: 1/16" - 1/8"

Attach to backside of the frame on dashed line.

SIERRA WETLANDS

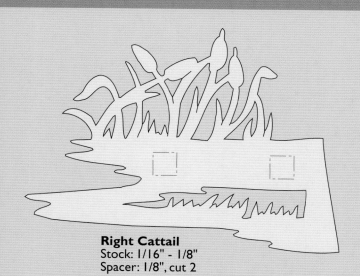

Right Cattail
Stock: 1/16" - 1/8"
Spacer: 1/8", cut 2

Fish
Stock: 1/16" - 1/8"
Spacer: 1/4", cut 2

Top Overlay
Stock: 1/16" - 1/8"

Bottom Overlay
Stock: 1/16" - 1/8"

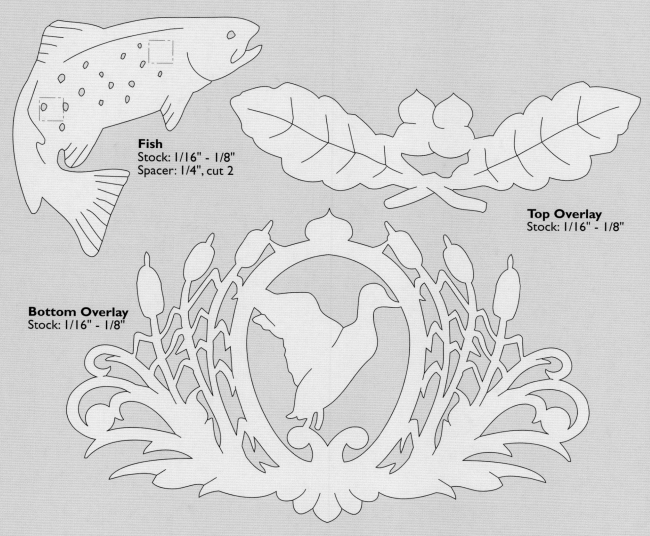

Sierra Wetlands

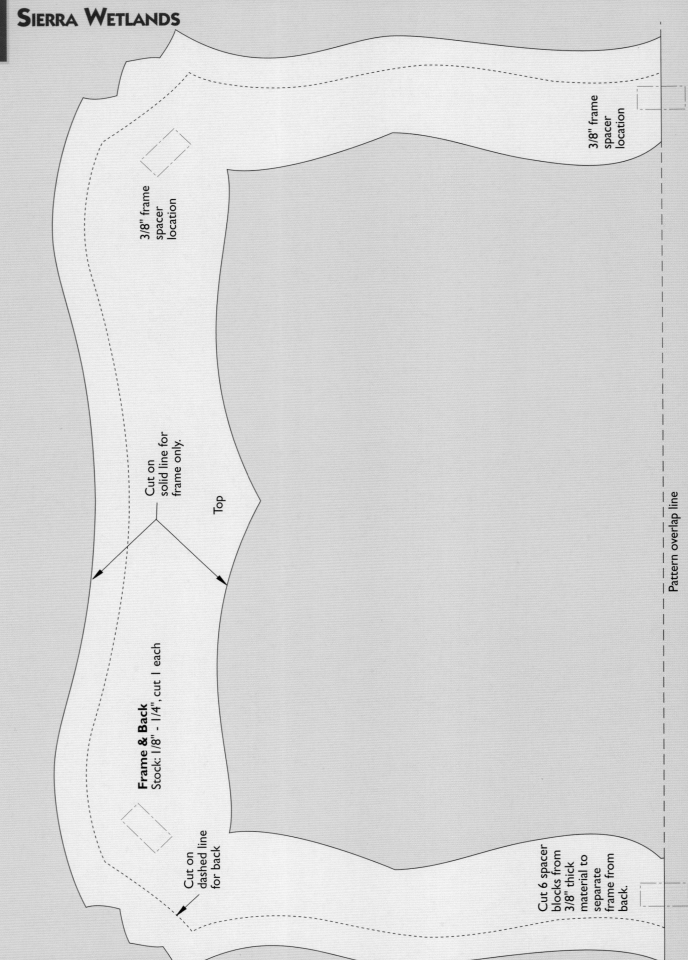

3/8" frame spacer location

3/8" frame spacer location

Cut on solid line for frame only.

Top

Frame & Back
Stock: 1/8" - 1/4", cut 1 each

Cut on dashed line for back

Cut 6 spacer blocks from 3/8" thick material to separate frame from back.

Pattern overlap line

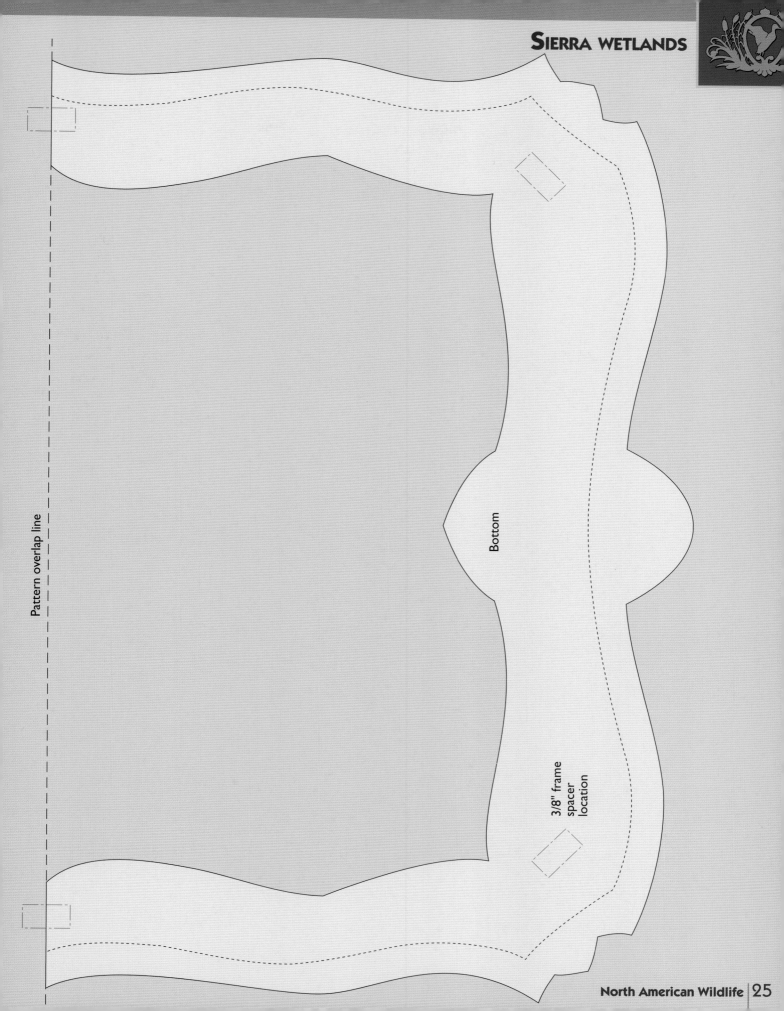

Pattern overlap line

Bottom

3/8" frame
spacer
location

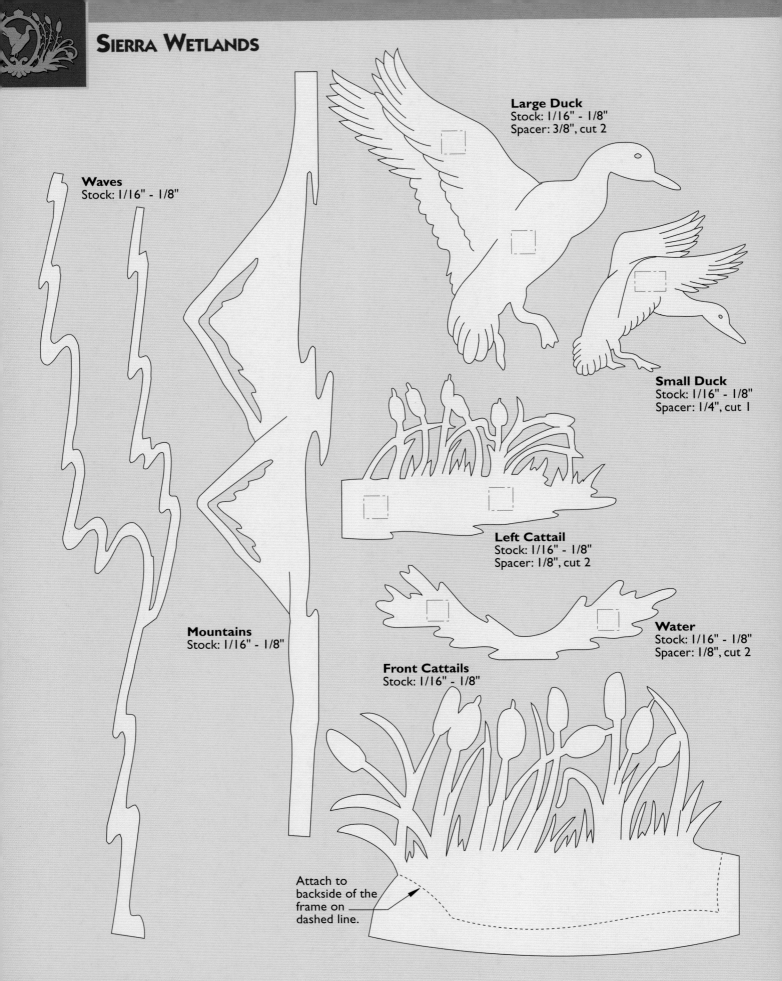

Sierra Wetlands

Waves
Stock: 1/16" - 1/8"

Large Duck
Stock: 1/16" - 1/8"
Spacer: 3/8", cut 2

Small Duck
Stock: 1/16" - 1/8"
Spacer: 1/4", cut 1

Left Cattail
Stock: 1/16" - 1/8"
Spacer: 1/8", cut 2

Mountains
Stock: 1/16" - 1/8"

Water
Stock: 1/16" - 1/8"
Spacer: 1/8", cut 2

Front Cattails
Stock: 1/16" - 1/8"

Attach to backside of the frame on dashed line.

Watchful Cougar

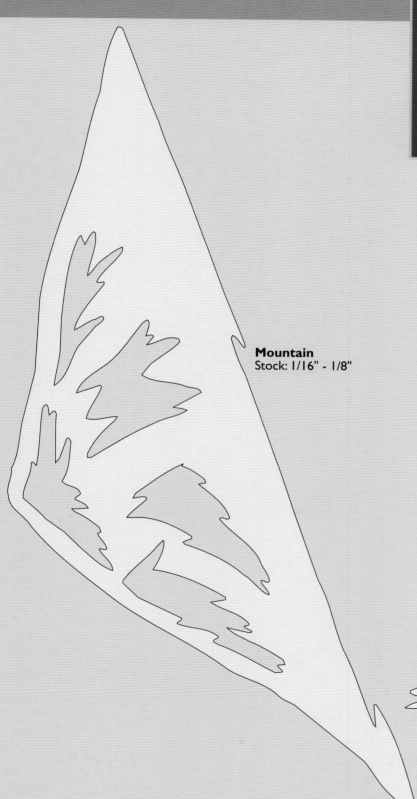

Mountain
Stock: 1/16" - 1/8"

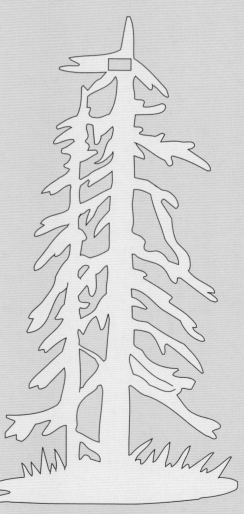

Right Trees
Stock: 1/16" - 1/8"
Spacer: 1/8", cut 2

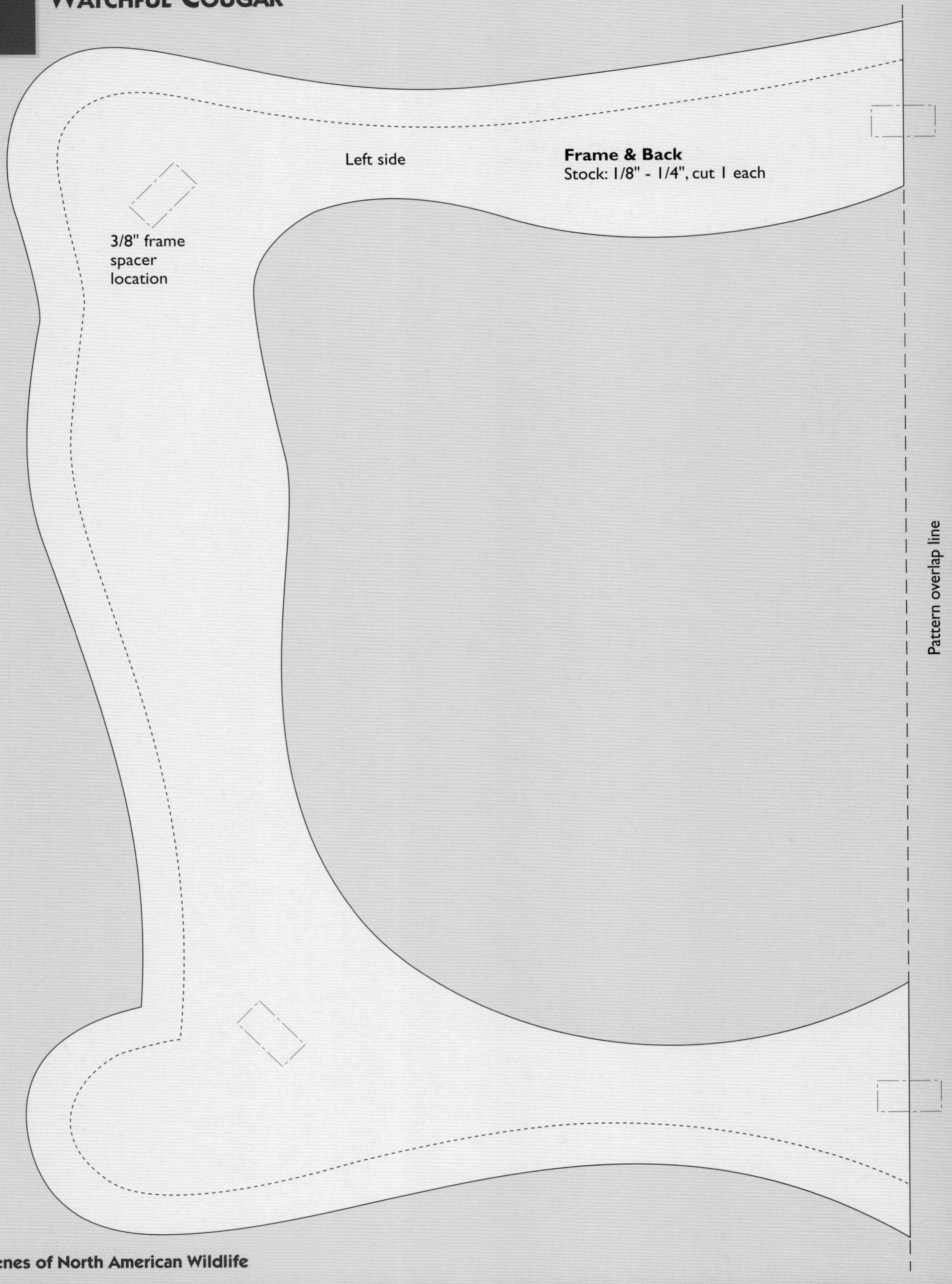

Left side

Frame & Back
Stock: 1/8" - 1/4", cut 1 each

3/8" frame
spacer
location

Pattern overlap line

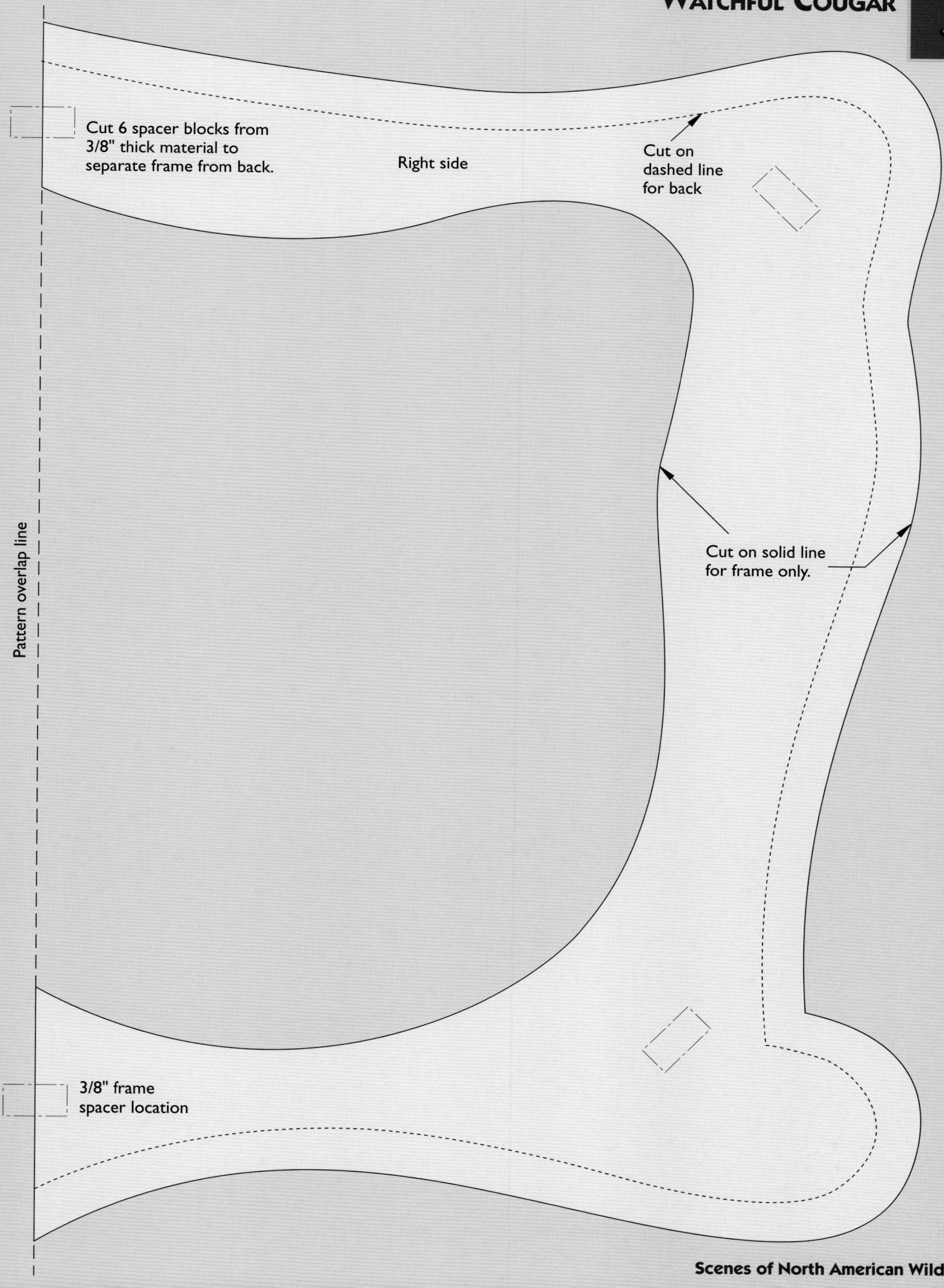

Cut 6 spacer blocks from
3/8" thick material to
separate frame from back.

Right side

Cut on
dashed line
for back

Cut on solid line
for frame only.

Pattern overlap line

3/8" frame
spacer location

WATCHFUL COUGAR

Eagle
Stock: 1/16" - 1/8"
Spacer: 1/8", cut 3

Left Tree
Stock: 1/16" - 1/8"
Spacer: 1/8", cut 2

Cougar
Stock: 1/16" - 1/8"
Spacer: 1/4", cut 3

Grass
Stock: 1/16" - 1/8"

Attach to backside of the
frame on dashed line.

CURIOUS

Small Cloud
Stock: 1/16" - 1/8"

Cloud
Stock: 1/16" - 1/8"
Spacer: 1/8", cut 2

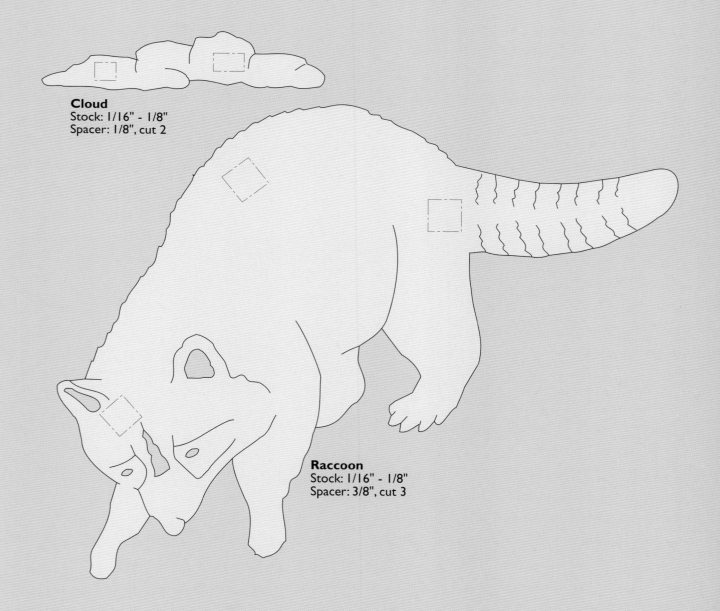

Raccoon
Stock: 1/16" - 1/8"
Spacer: 3/8", cut 3

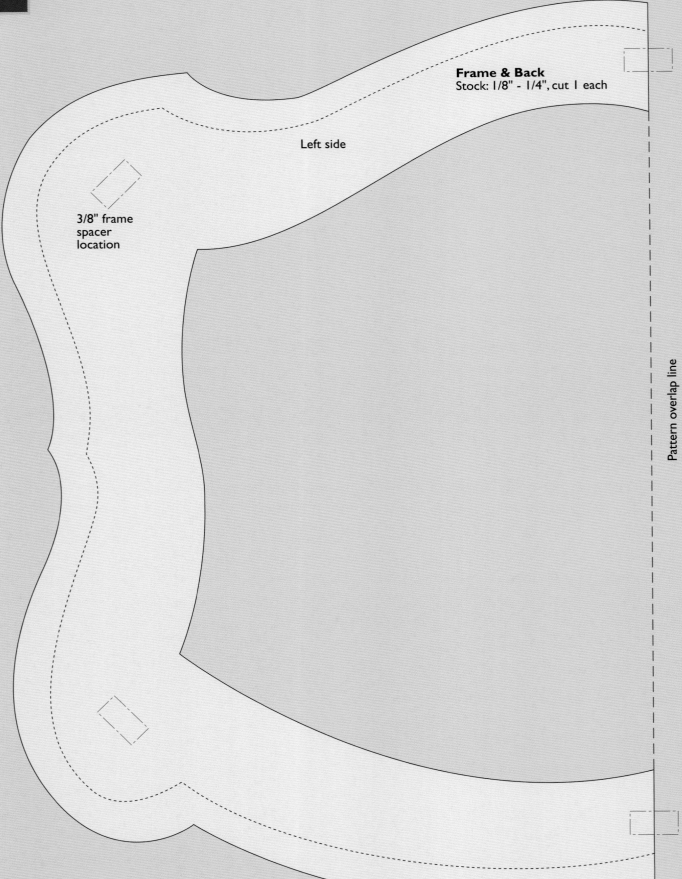

Frame & Back
Stock: 1/8" - 1/4", cut 1 each

Left side

3/8" frame
spacer
location

Pattern overlap line

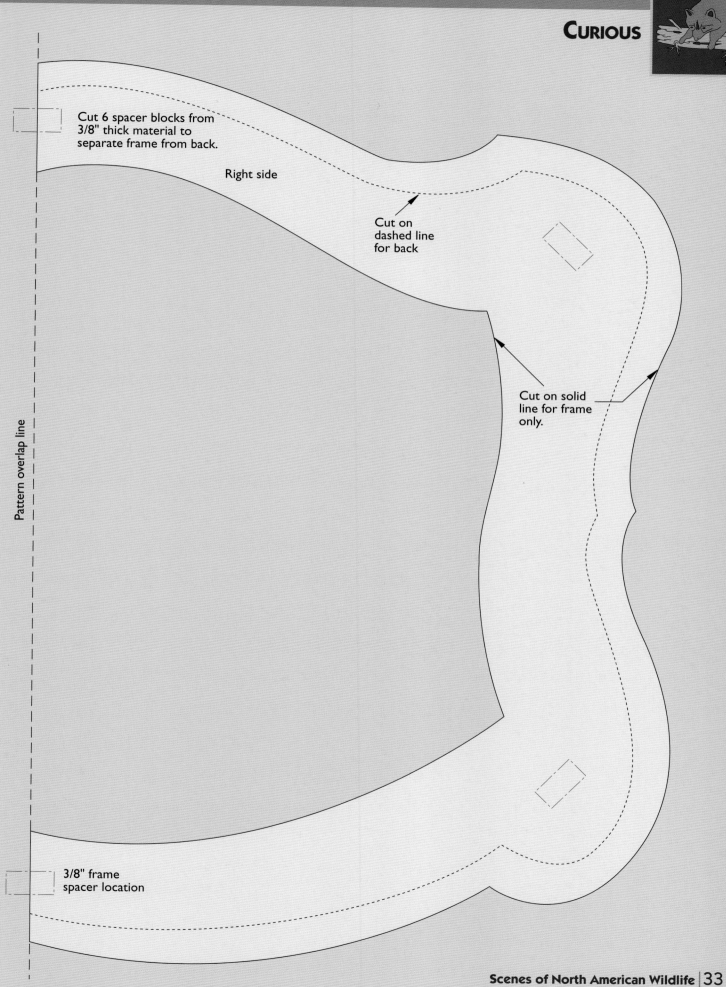

Cut 6 spacer blocks from 3/8" thick material to separate frame from back.

Right side

Cut on dashed line for back

Cut on solid line for frame only.

Pattern overlap line

3/8" frame spacer location

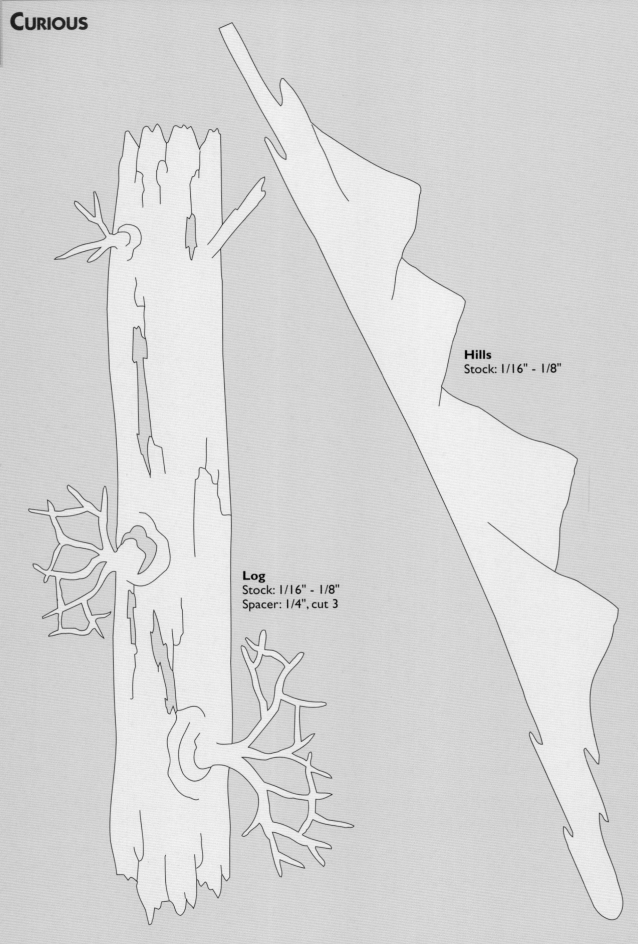

Hills
Stock: 1/16" - 1/8"

Log
Stock: 1/16" - 1/8"
Spacer: 1/4", cut 3

GOD'S COUNTRY

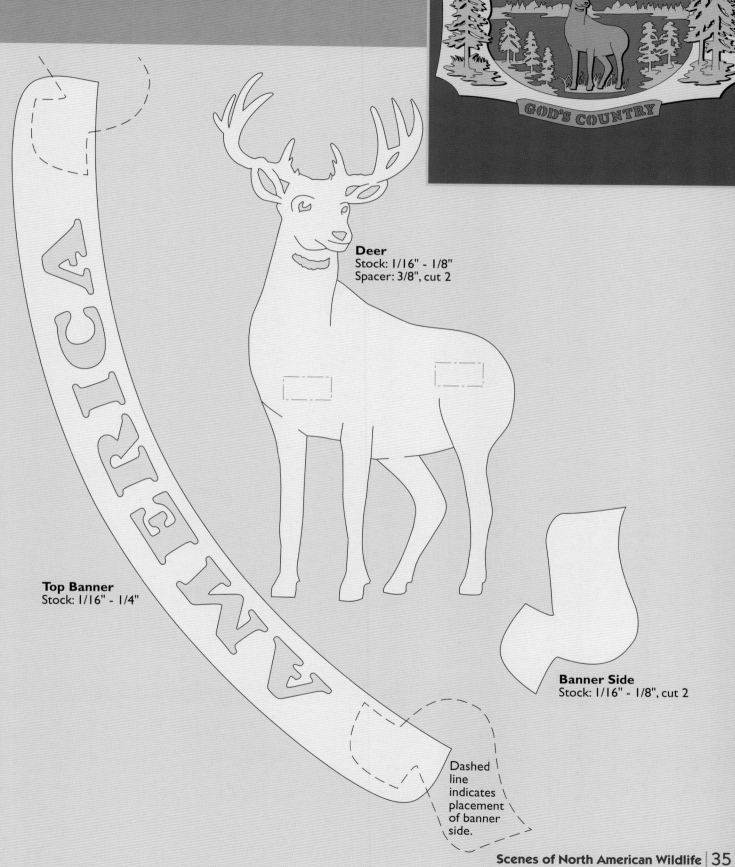

Deer
Stock: 1/16" - 1/8"
Spacer: 3/8", cut 2

Top Banner
Stock: 1/16" - 1/4"

Banner Side
Stock: 1/16" - 1/8", cut 2

Dashed line indicates placement of banner side.

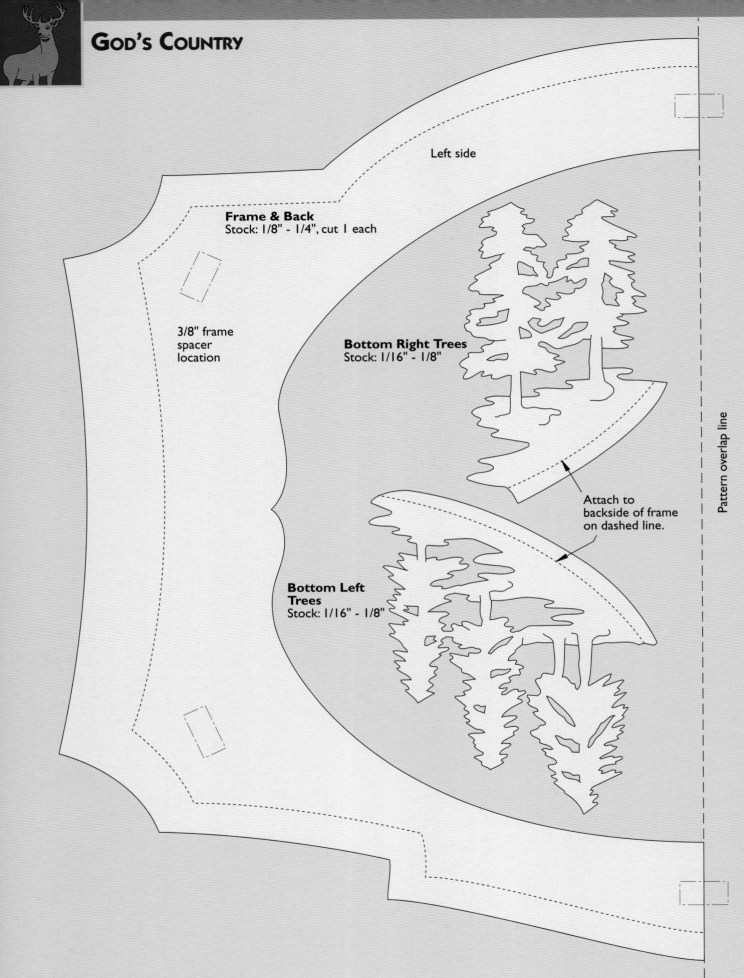

Frame & Back
Stock: 1/8" - 1/4", cut 1 each

Left side

3/8" frame
spacer
location

Bottom Right Trees
Stock: 1/16" - 1/8"

Attach to
backside of frame
on dashed line.

**Bottom Left
Trees**
Stock: 1/16" - 1/8"

Pattern overlap line

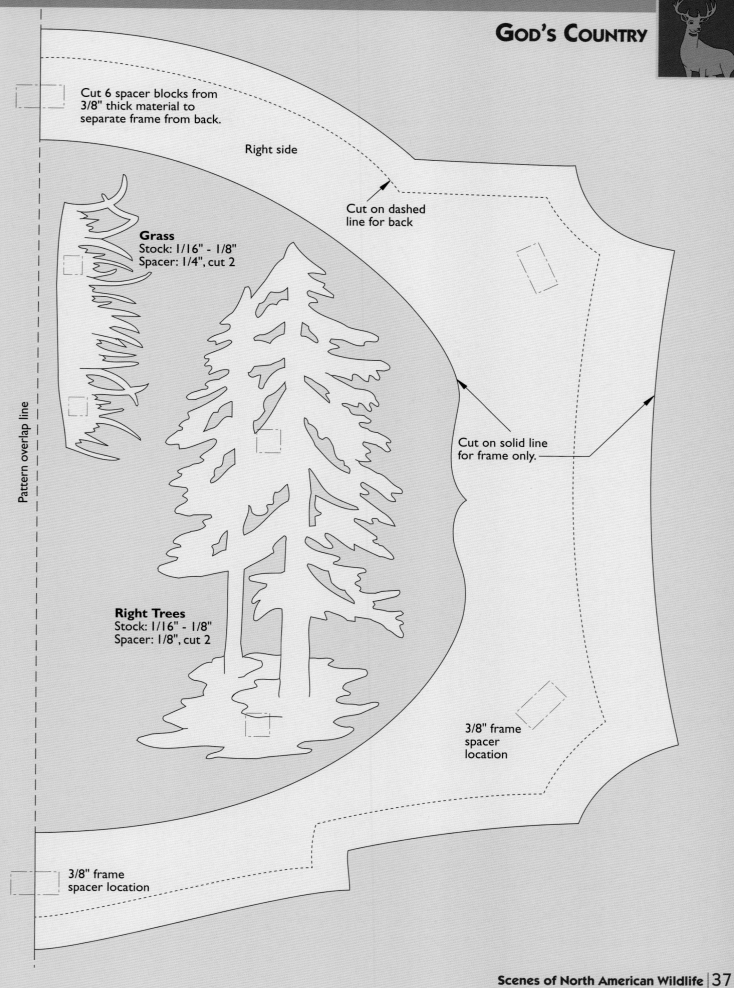

Cut 6 spacer blocks from 3/8" thick material to separate frame from back.

Right side

Cut on dashed line for back

Grass
Stock: 1/16" - 1/8"
Spacer: 1/4", cut 2

Pattern overlap line

Cut on solid line for frame only.

Right Trees
Stock: 1/16" - 1/8"
Spacer: 1/8", cut 2

3/8" frame spacer location

3/8" frame spacer location

GOD'S COUNTRY

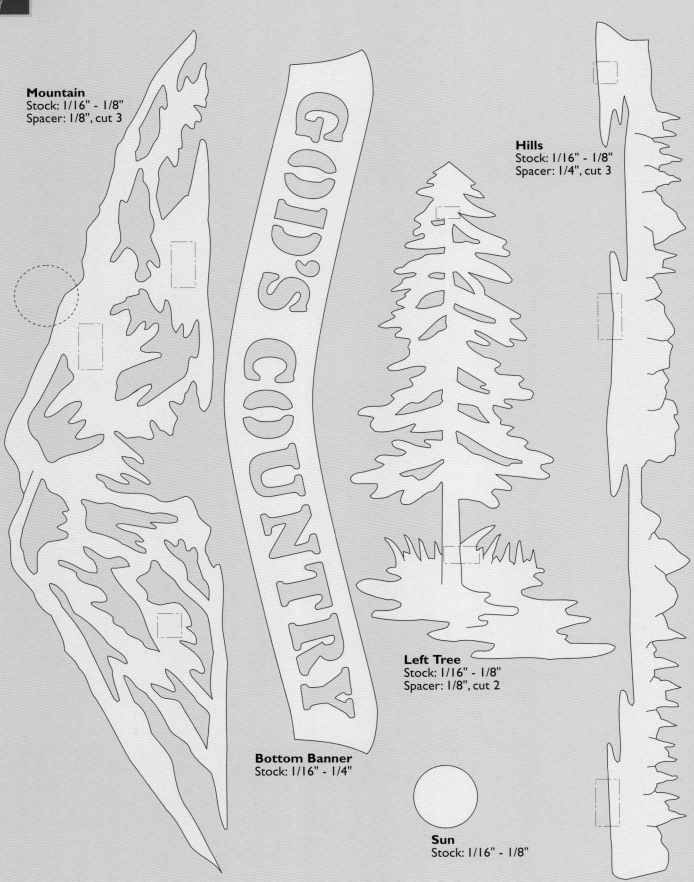

Mountain
Stock: 1/16" - 1/8"
Spacer: 1/8", cut 3

Hills
Stock: 1/16" - 1/8"
Spacer: 1/4", cut 3

Left Tree
Stock: 1/16" - 1/8"
Spacer: 1/8", cut 2

Bottom Banner
Stock: 1/16" - 1/4"

Sun
Stock: 1/16" - 1/8"

DEER'S PATH

Right Eagle
Stock: 1/16" - 1/8"
Spacer: 1/8", cut 3

Right Mountain
Stock: 1/16" - 1/8"

Right Back Tree
Stock: 1/16" - 1/8"
Spacer: 1/8", cut 2

Right Trees
Stock: 1/16" - 1/8"
Spacer: 1/8", cut 3

Back Grass
Stock: 1/16" - 1/8"

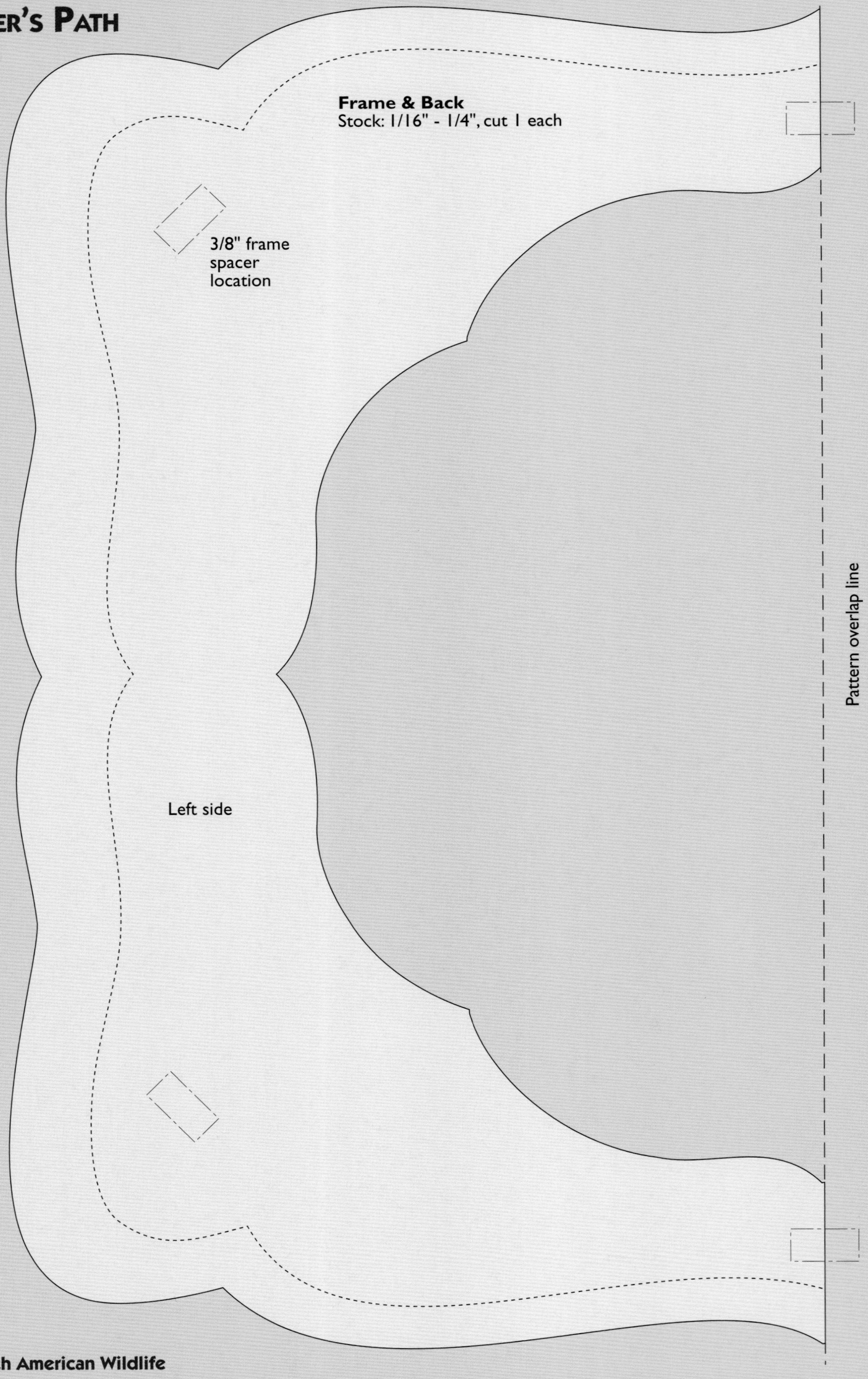

Frame & Back
Stock: 1/16" - 1/4", cut 1 each

3/8" frame
spacer
location

Left side

Pattern overlap line

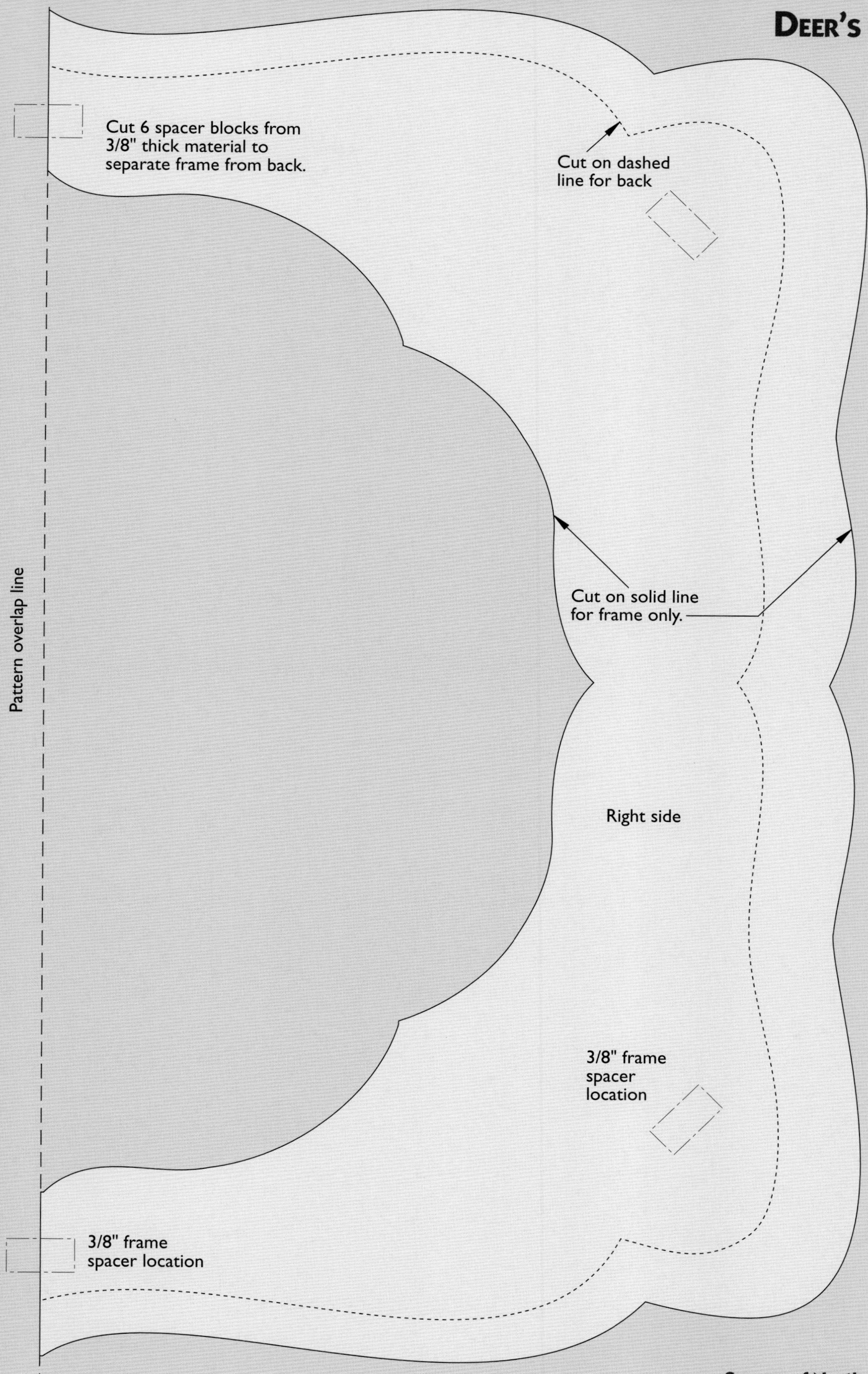

Cut 6 spacer blocks from
3/8" thick material to
separate frame from back.

Cut on dashed
line for back

Cut on solid line
for frame only.

Right side

3/8" frame
spacer
location

Pattern overlap line

3/8" frame
spacer location

DEER'S PATH

Left Eagle
Stock: 1/16" - 1/8"
Spacer: 1/8", cut 2

Left Back Trees
Stock: 1/16" - 1/8"

Small Mountain
Stock: 1/16" - 1/8"

Front Cloud
Stock: 1/16" - 1/8"
Spacer: 1/8", cut 1

Back Cloud
Stock: 1/16" - 1/8"

Overlay
Stock: 1/16" - 1/8"

Deer
Stock: 1/16" - 1/8"
Spacer: 1/4", cut 3

Left Front Tree
Stock: 1/16" - 1/8"
Spacer: 1/8", cut 3

Attach to backside
of the frame on
dashed line.

Front Grass
Stock: 1/16" - 1/8"

DEER PORTRAIT

Drake
Stock: 1/16" - 1/8"
Spacer: 1/8", cut 2

Grass
Stock: 1/16" - 1/8"

Attach to backside
of the frame on
dashed line.

Side Grass
Stock: 1/16" - 1/8"
Spacer: 1/8", cut 1

Eagle
Stock: 1/16" - 1/8"
Spacer: 1/8", cut 3

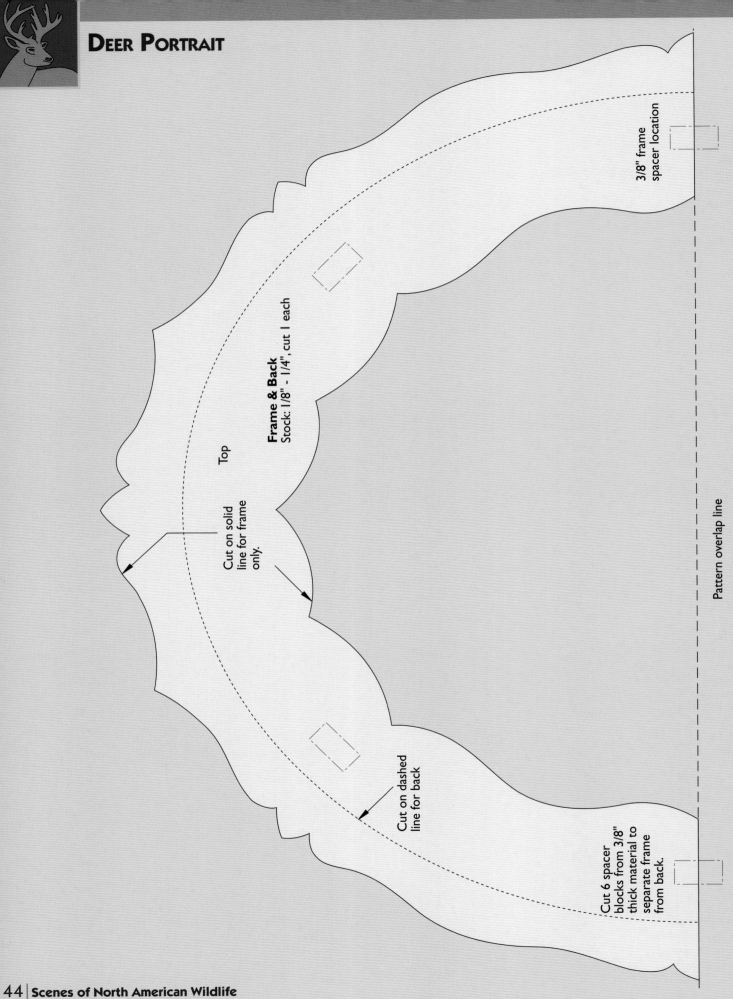

3/8" frame spacer location

Frame & Back
Stock: 1/8" - 1/4", cut 1 each

Top

Cut on solid line for frame only.

Cut on dashed line for back

Cut 6 spacer blocks from 3/8" thick material to separate frame from back.

Pattern overlap line

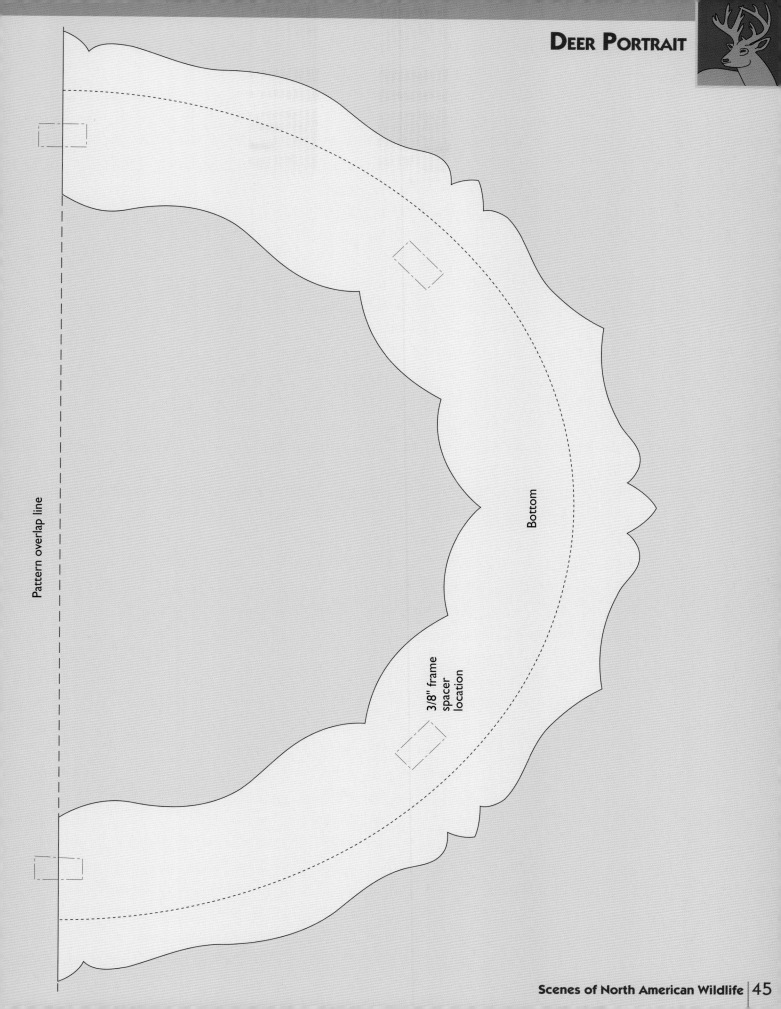

Pattern overlap line

3/8" frame
spacer
location

Bottom

Deer Portrait

Mountains
Stock: 1/16" - 1/8"

Sun
Stock: 1/16" - 1/8"

Cloud
Stock: 1/16" - 1/8"
Spacer: 1/8", cut 1

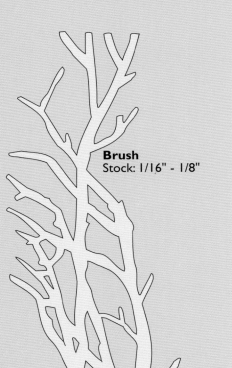

Brush
Stock: 1/16" - 1/8"

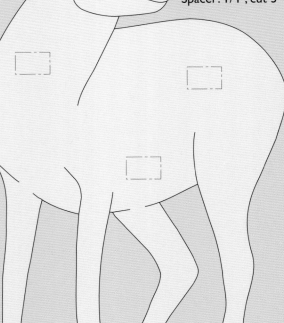

Deer
Stock: 1/16" - 1/8"
Spacer: 1/4", cut 3

Leaps and Bounds

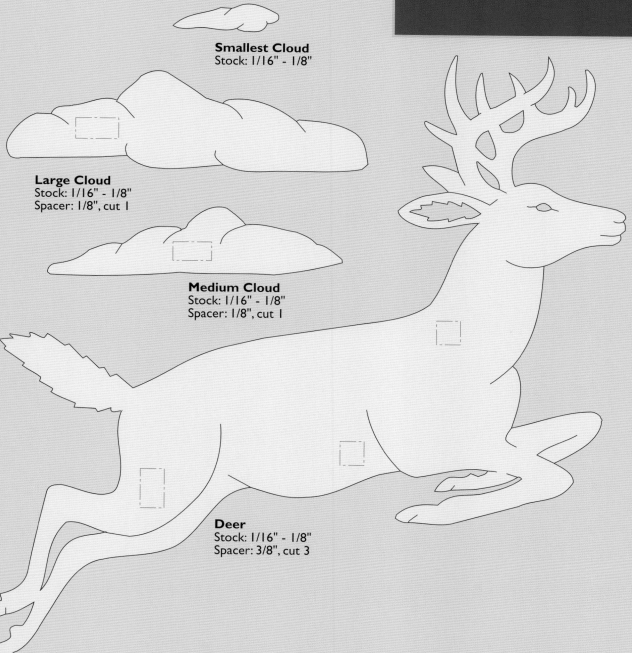

Smallest Cloud
Stock: 1/16" - 1/8"

Large Cloud
Stock: 1/16" - 1/8"
Spacer: 1/8", cut 1

Medium Cloud
Stock: 1/16" - 1/8"
Spacer: 1/8", cut 1

Deer
Stock: 1/16" - 1/8"
Spacer: 3/8", cut 3

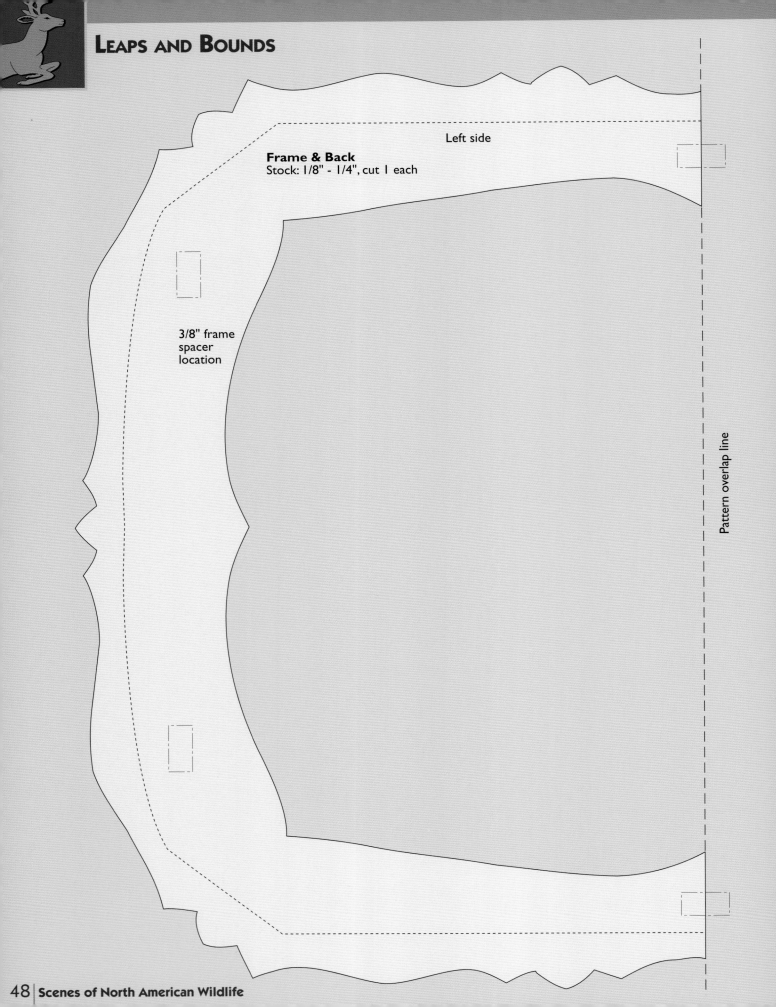

Left side

Frame & Back
Stock: 1/8" - 1/4", cut 1 each

3/8" frame
spacer
location

Pattern overlap line

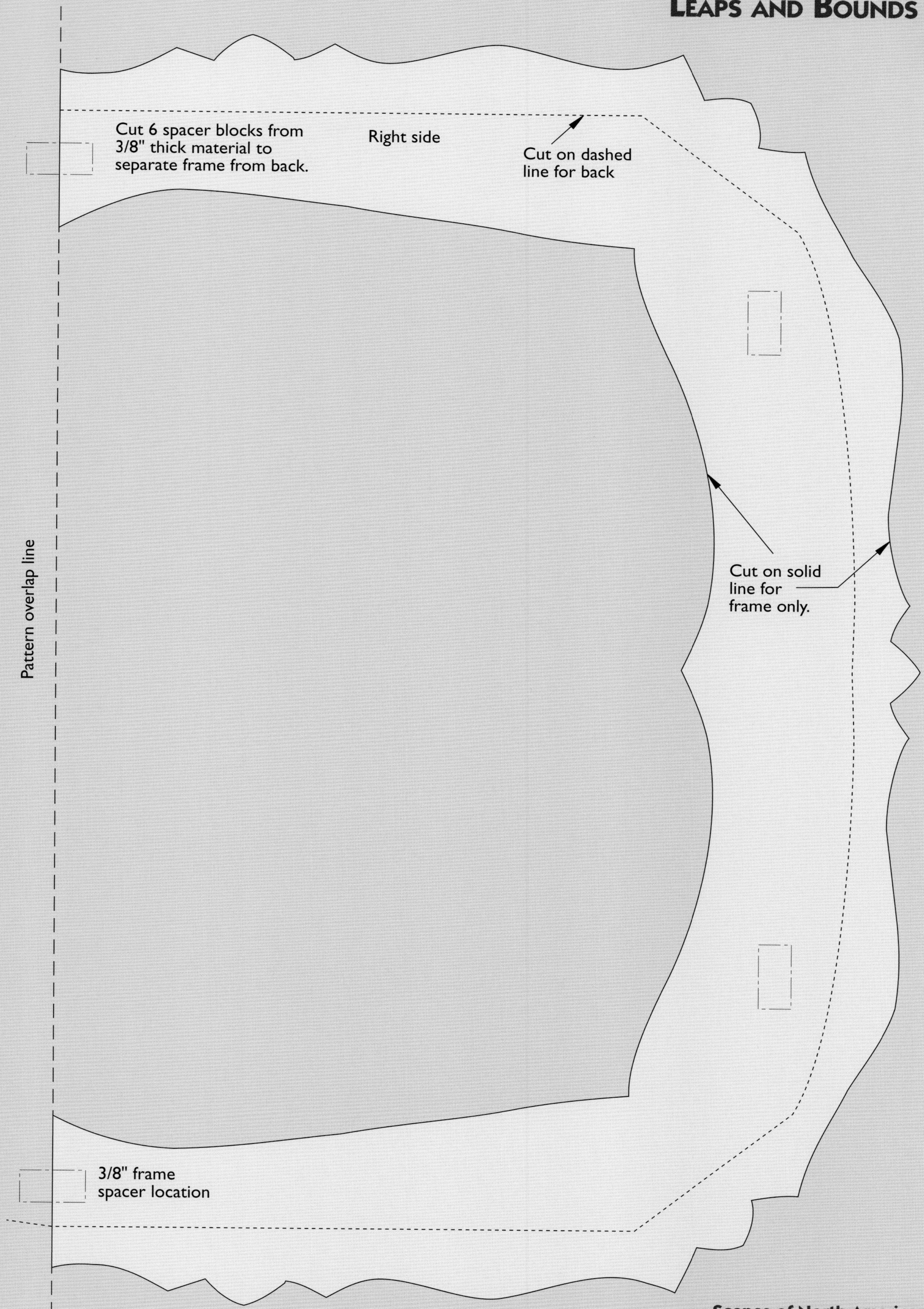

Cut 6 spacer blocks from
3/8" thick material to
separate frame from back.

Right side

Cut on dashed
line for back

Pattern overlap line

Cut on solid
line for
frame only.

3/8" frame
spacer location

LEAPS AND BOUNDS

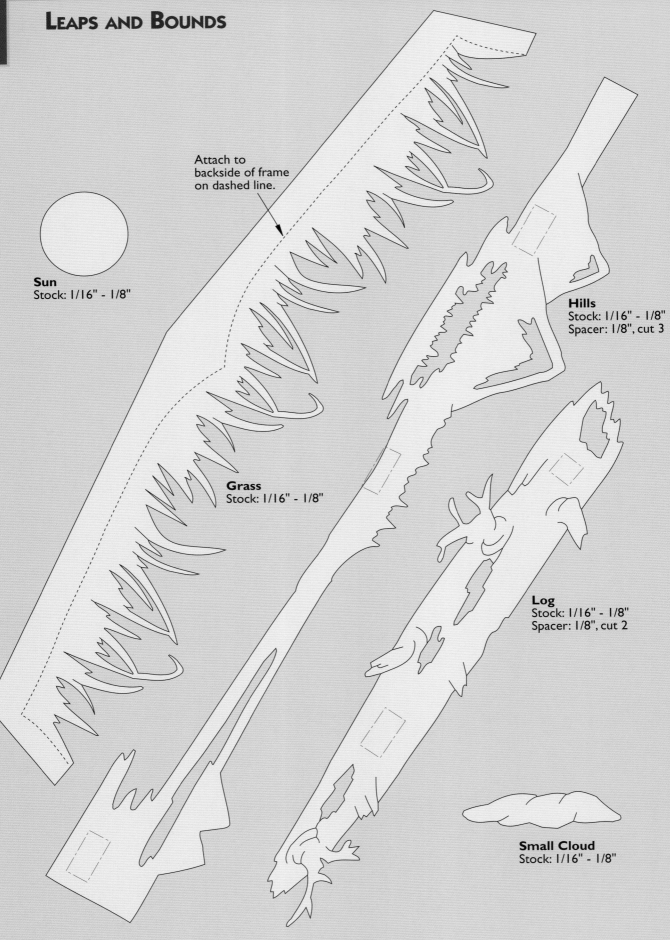

Attach to backside of frame on dashed line.

Sun
Stock: 1/16" - 1/8"

Hills
Stock: 1/16" - 1/8"
Spacer: 1/8", cut 3

Grass
Stock: 1/16" - 1/8"

Log
Stock: 1/16" - 1/8"
Spacer: 1/8", cut 2

Small Cloud
Stock: 1/16" - 1/8"

MEADOW REST

Right Meadow
Stock: 1/16" - 1/8"
Spacer: 1/8", cut 4

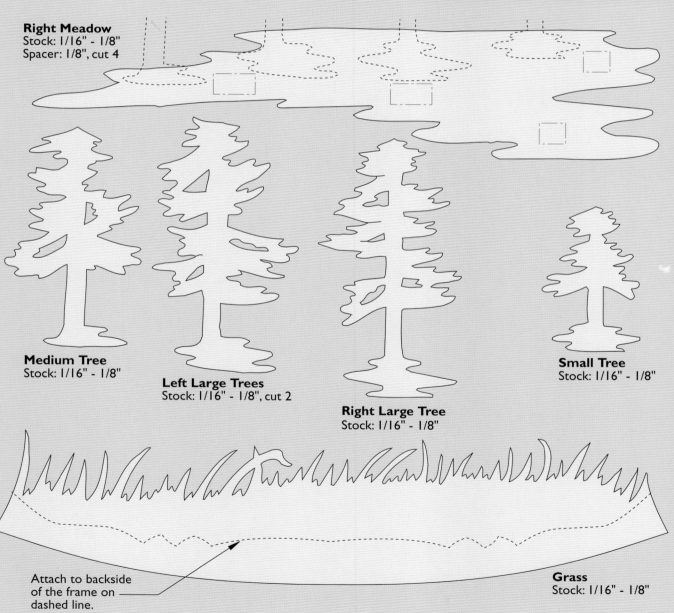

Medium Tree
Stock: 1/16" - 1/8"

Left Large Trees
Stock: 1/16" - 1/8", cut 2

Right Large Tree
Stock: 1/16" - 1/8"

Small Tree
Stock: 1/16" - 1/8"

Attach to backside
of the frame on
dashed line.

Grass
Stock: 1/16" - 1/8"

Meadow Rest

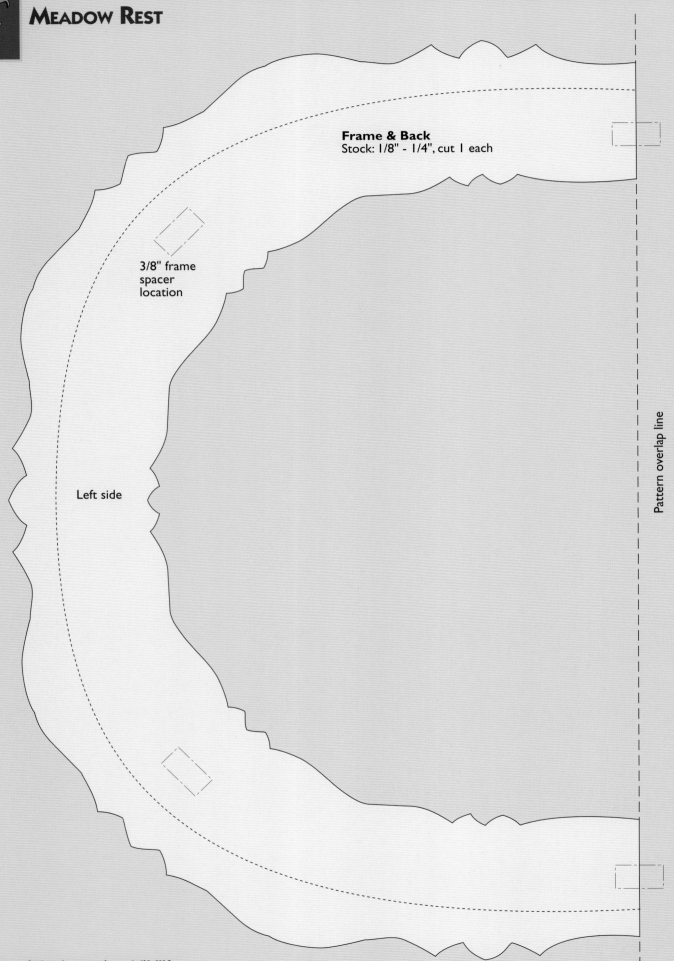

Frame & Back
Stock: 1/8" - 1/4", cut 1 each

3/8" frame
spacer
location

Left side

Pattern overlap line

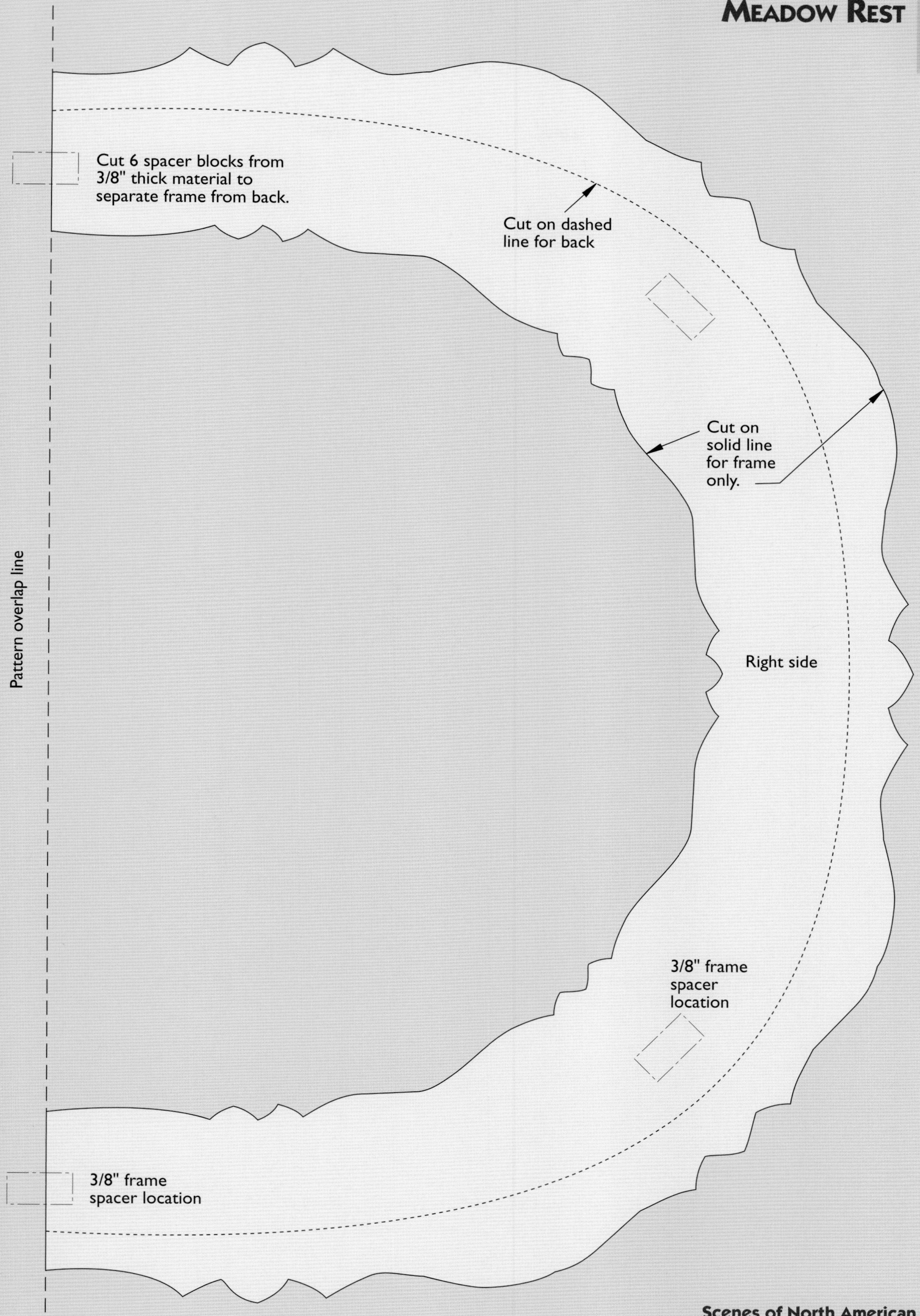

Cut 6 spacer blocks from
3/8" thick material to
separate frame from back.

Cut on dashed
line for back

Cut on
solid line
for frame
only.

Right side

3/8" frame
spacer
location

Pattern overlap line

3/8" frame
spacer location

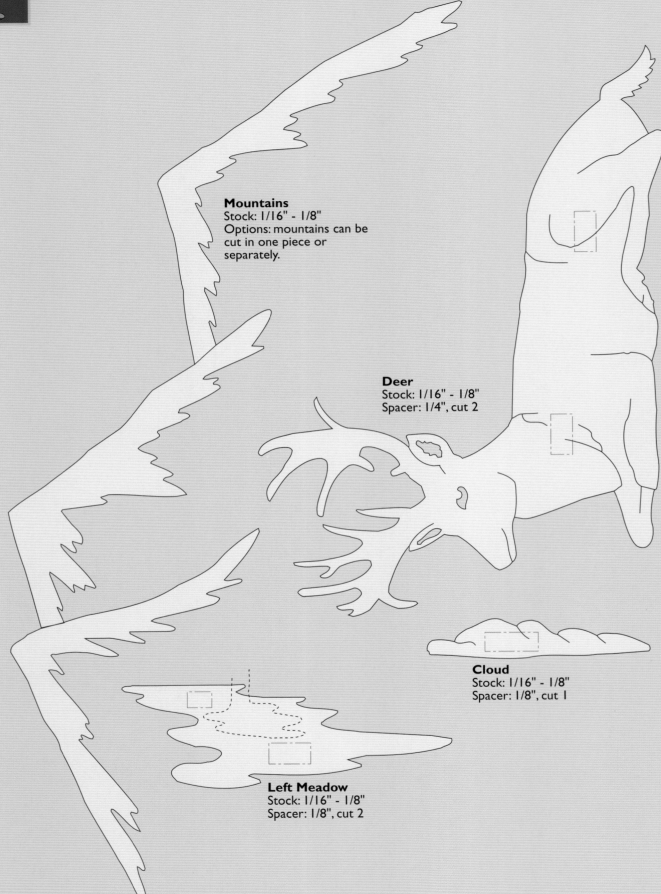

Mountains
Stock: 1/16" - 1/8"
Options: mountains can be
cut in one piece or
separately.

Deer
Stock: 1/16" - 1/8"
Spacer: 1/4", cut 2

Cloud
Stock: 1/16" - 1/8"
Spacer: 1/8", cut 1

Left Meadow
Stock: 1/16" - 1/8"
Spacer: 1/8", cut 2

DEER PAIR

Right Tree
Stock: 1/16" - 1/8"
Spacer: 1/8", cut 2

Overlay
Stock: 1/16" - 1/8"

Back Grass
Stock: 1/16" - 1/8"

Right Deer
Stock: 1/16" - 1/8"
Spacer: 3/8", cut 2

Center Grass
Stock: 1/16" - 1/8"

Right Stump
Stock: 1/16" - 1/8"

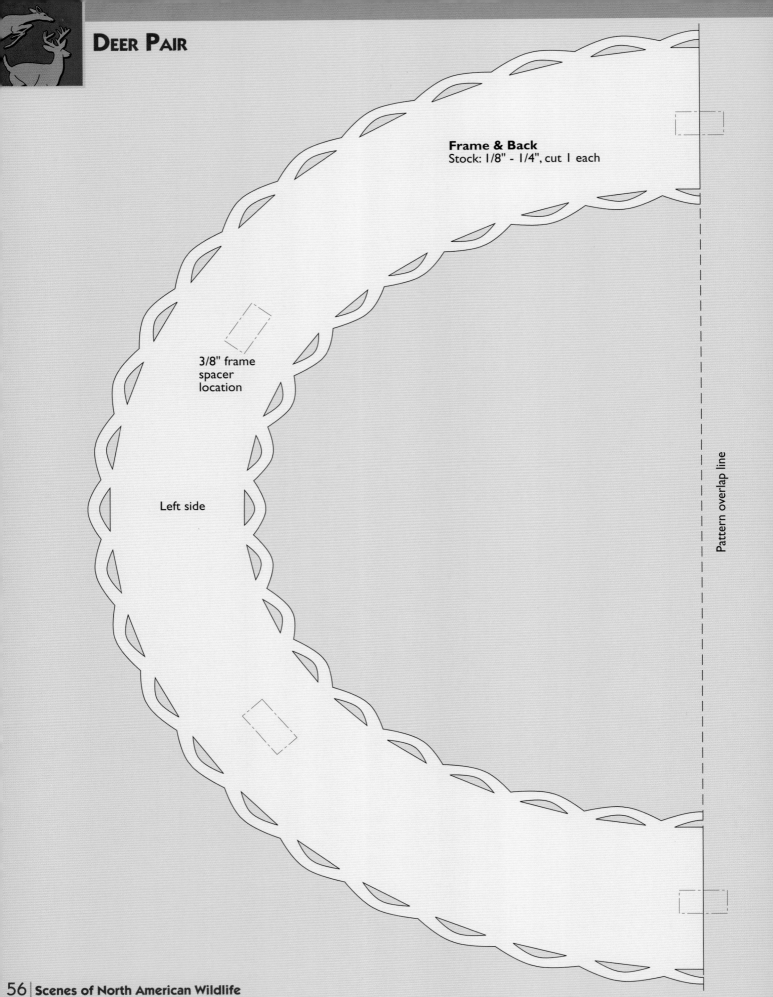

Frame & Back
Stock: 1/8" - 1/4", cut 1 each

3/8" frame
spacer
location

Left side

Pattern overlap line

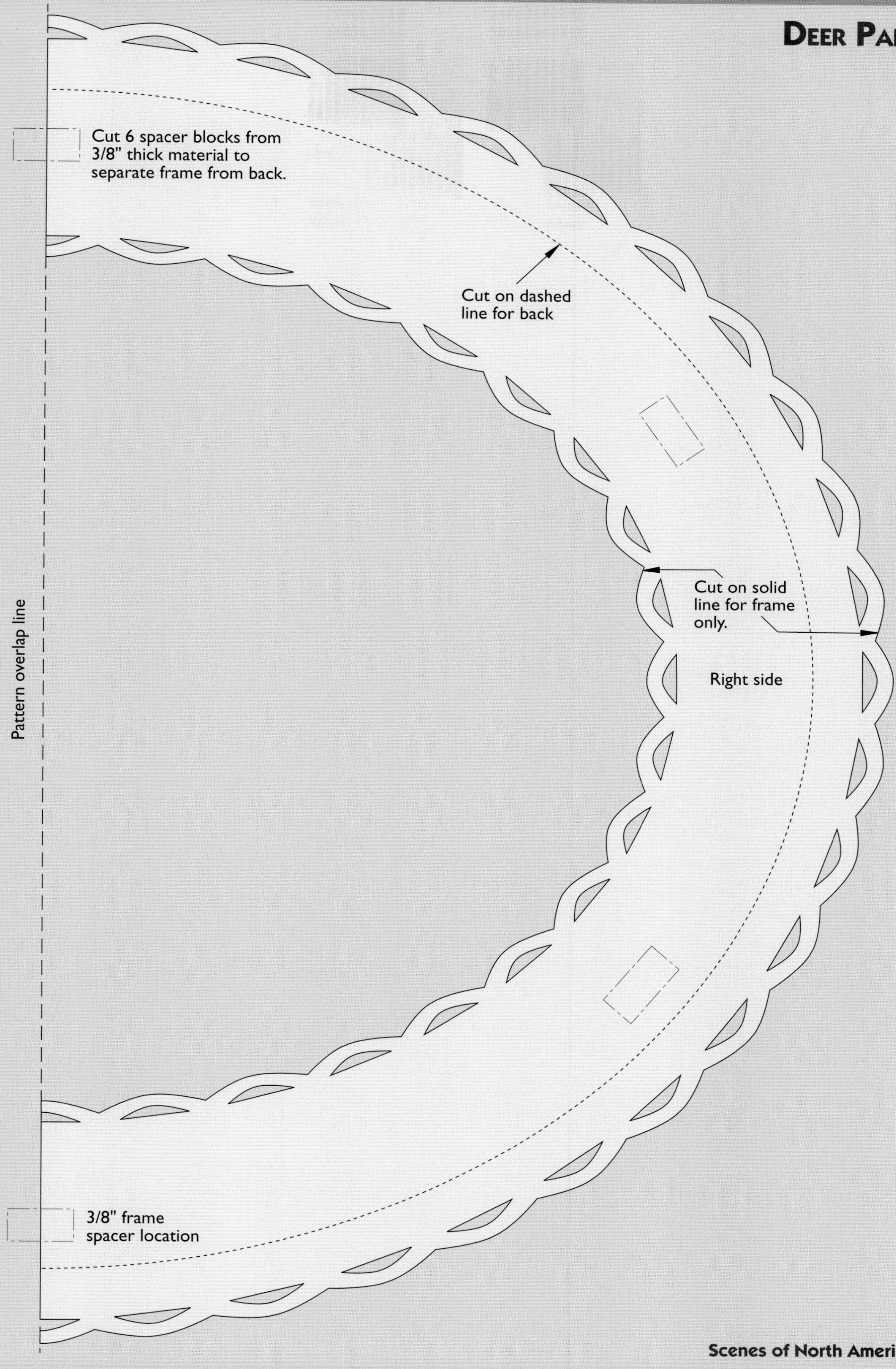

Cut 6 spacer blocks from
3/8" thick material to
separate frame from back.

Cut on dashed
line for back

Cut on solid
line for frame
only.

Right side

Pattern overlap line

3/8" frame
spacer location

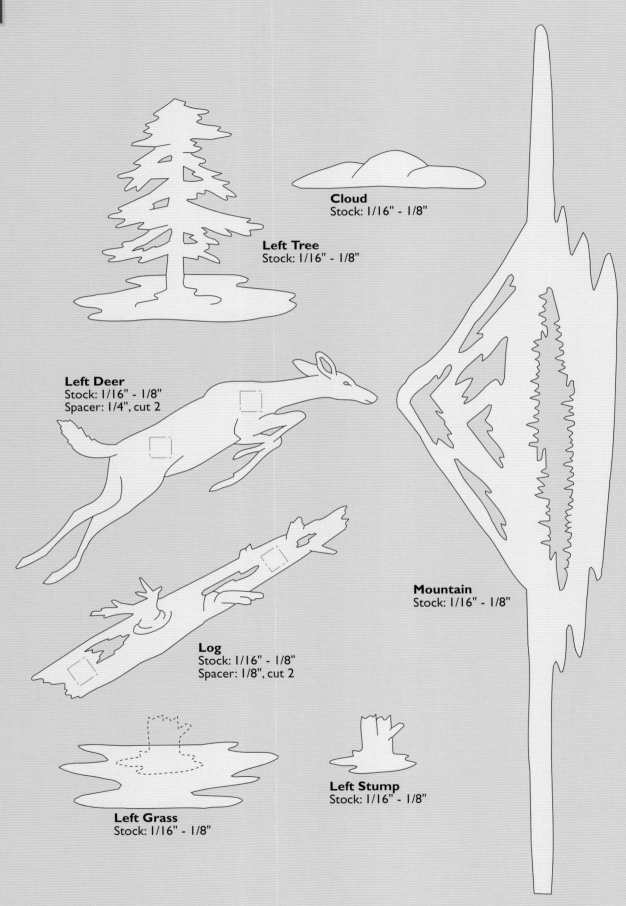

Cloud
Stock: 1/16" - 1/8"

Left Tree
Stock: 1/16" - 1/8"

Left Deer
Stock: 1/16" - 1/8"
Spacer: 1/4", cut 2

Mountain
Stock: 1/16" - 1/8"

Log
Stock: 1/16" - 1/8"
Spacer: 1/8", cut 2

Left Stump
Stock: 1/16" - 1/8"

Left Grass
Stock: 1/16" - 1/8"

ELK CALL

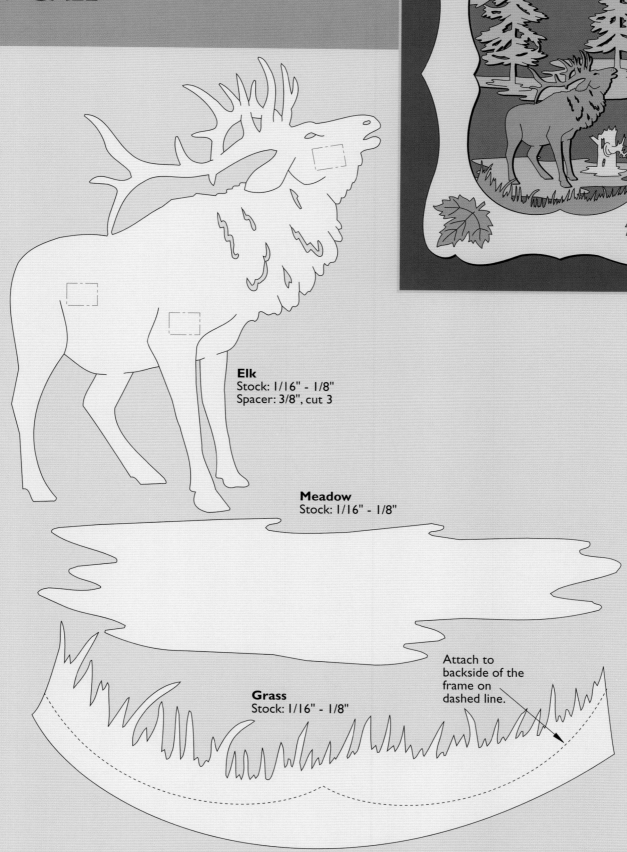

Elk
Stock: 1/16" - 1/8"
Spacer: 3/8", cut 3

Meadow
Stock: 1/16" - 1/8"

Grass
Stock: 1/16" - 1/8"

Attach to backside of the frame on dashed line.

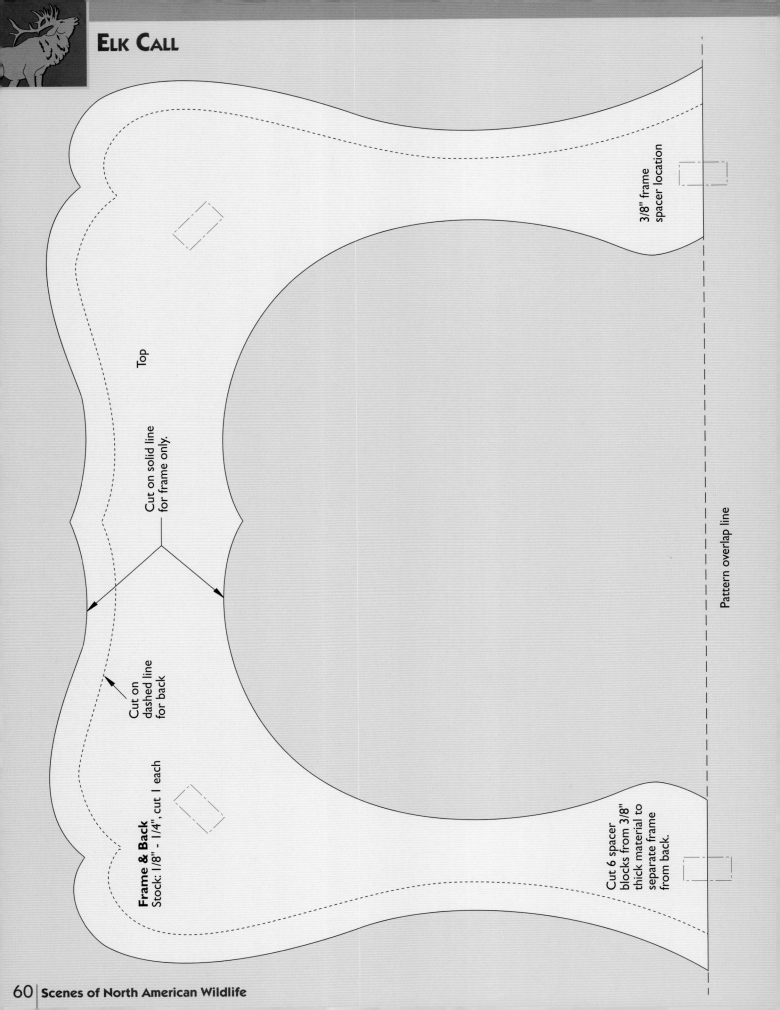

ELK CALL

Top

Cut on solid line
for frame only.

Cut on
dashed line
for back

Frame & Back
Stock: 1/8" - 1/4", cut 1 each

3/8" frame
spacer location

Pattern overlap line

Cut 6 spacer
blocks from 3/8"
thick material to
separate frame
from back.

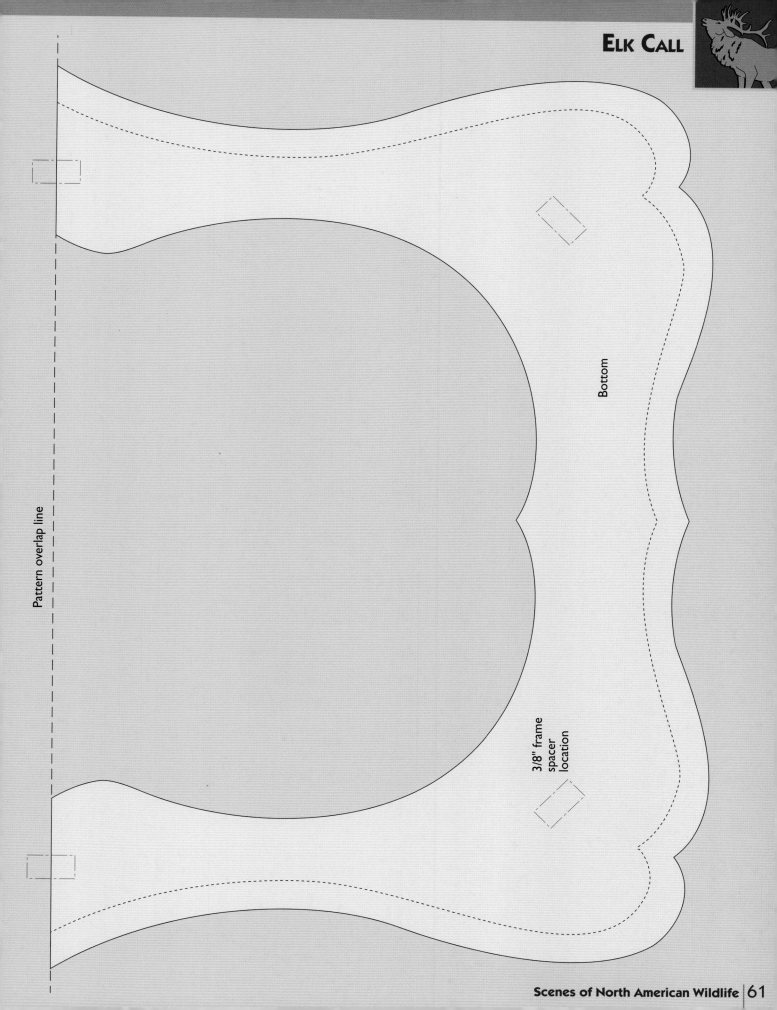

Pattern overlap line

Bottom

3/8" frame
spacer
location

ELK CALL

Cloud
Stock: 1/16" - 1/8"
Spacer: 1/8", cut 1

Back Mountain
Stock: 1/16" - 1/8"

Leaf
Stock: 1/16" - 1/8", cut 4

Mountain
Stock: 1/16" - 1/8"

Stump
Stock: 1/16" - 1/8"
Spacer: 1/8", cut 1

Trees
Stock: 1/16" - 1/8"
Spacer: 1/8", cut 4

ELK AT REST

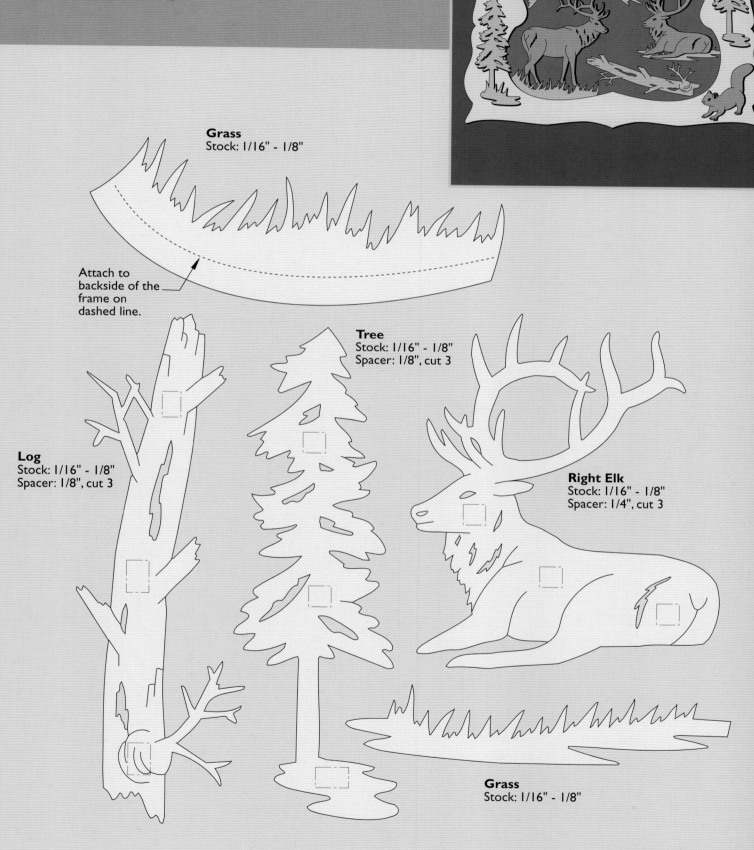

Grass
Stock: 1/16" - 1/8"

Attach to backside of the frame on dashed line.

Log
Stock: 1/16" - 1/8"
Spacer: 1/8", cut 3

Tree
Stock: 1/16" - 1/8"
Spacer: 1/8", cut 3

Right Elk
Stock: 1/16" - 1/8"
Spacer: 1/4", cut 3

Grass
Stock: 1/16" - 1/8"

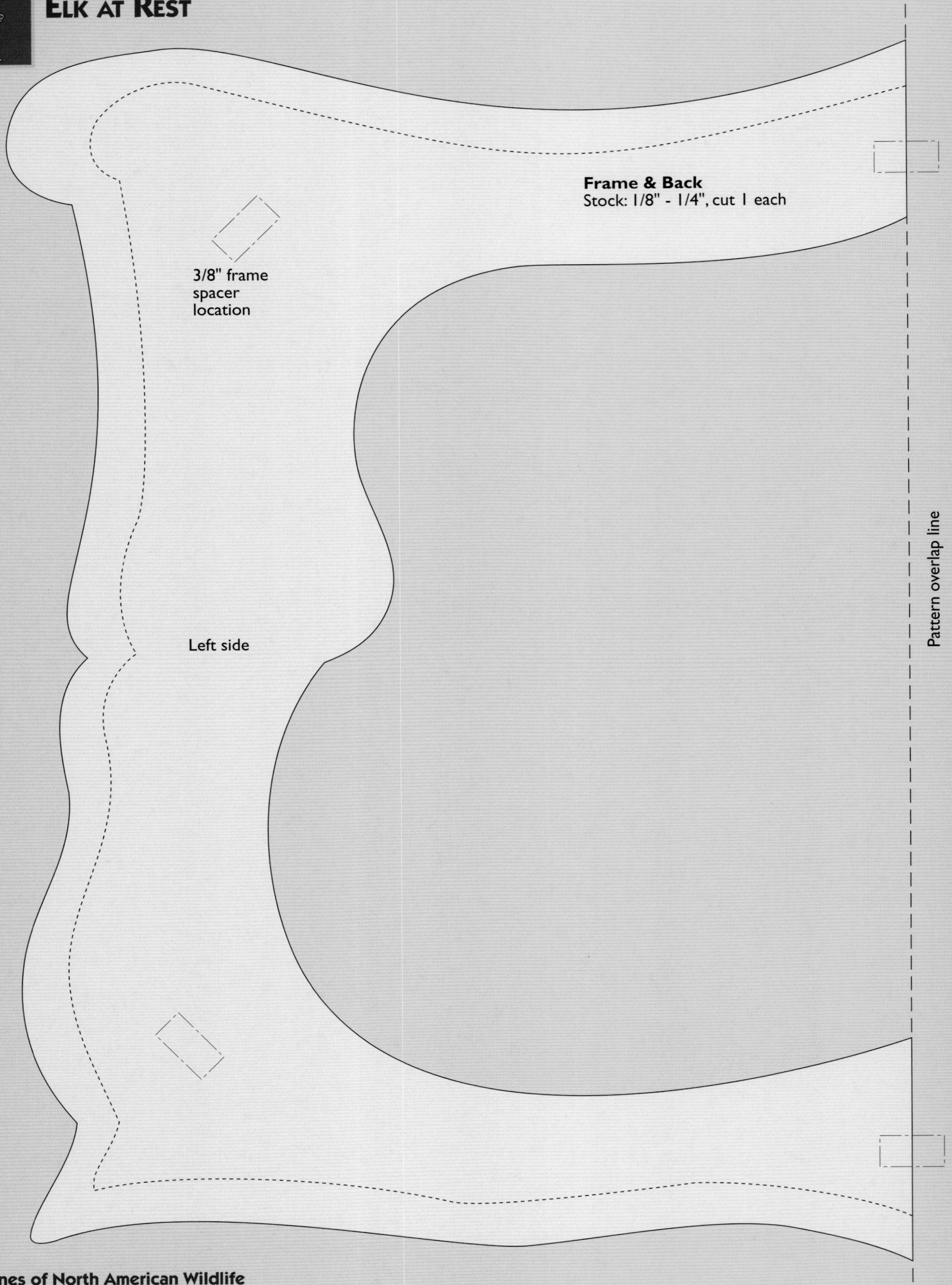

Frame & Back
Stock: 1/8" - 1/4", cut 1 each

3/8" frame
spacer
location

Left side

Pattern overlap line

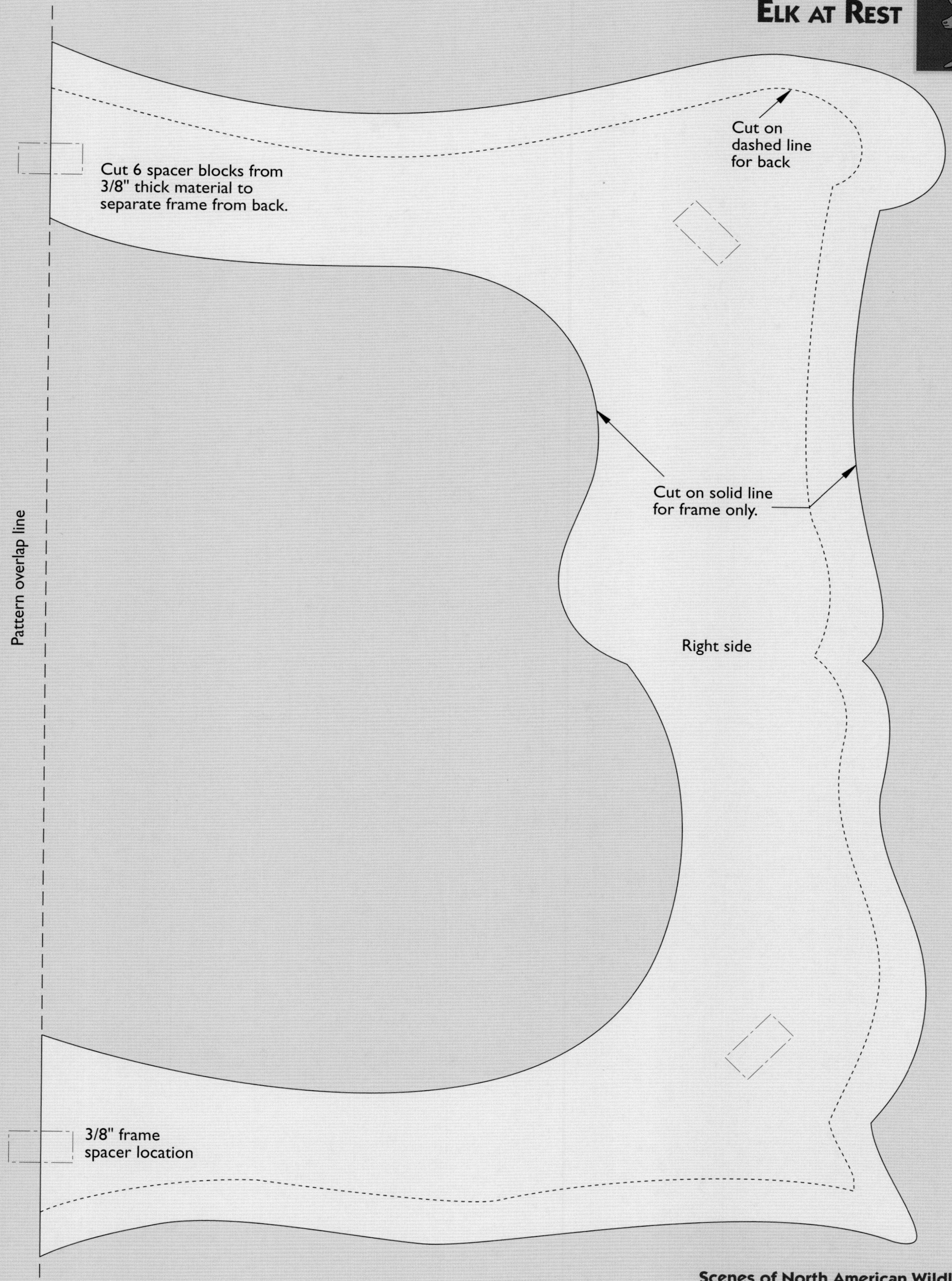

Cut on
dashed line
for back

Cut 6 spacer blocks from
3/8" thick material to
separate frame from back.

Cut on solid line
for frame only.

Right side

Pattern overlap line

3/8" frame
spacer location

ELK AT REST

Mountain
Stock: 1/16" - 1/8"

Elk
Stock: 1/16" - 1/8"
Spacer: 1/4", cut 3

Back Mountain
Stock: 1/16" - 1/8"

Left Tree
Stock: 1/16" - 1/8"
Spacer: 1/8", cut 3

Squirrel
Stock: 1/16" - 1/8"
Spacer: 1/8", cut 3

Eagle
Stock: 1/16" - 1/8"
Spacer: 1/8", cut 3

ELK PORTRAIT

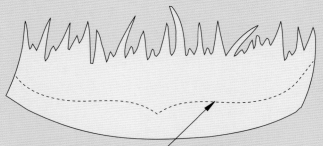

Attach to backside
of the frame on
dashed line.

Grass
Stock: 1/16" - 1/8"

Right Tree
Stock: 1/16" - 1/8"
Spacer: 1/8", cut 3

Left Tree
Stock: 1/16" - 1/8"
Spacer: 1/8", cut 3

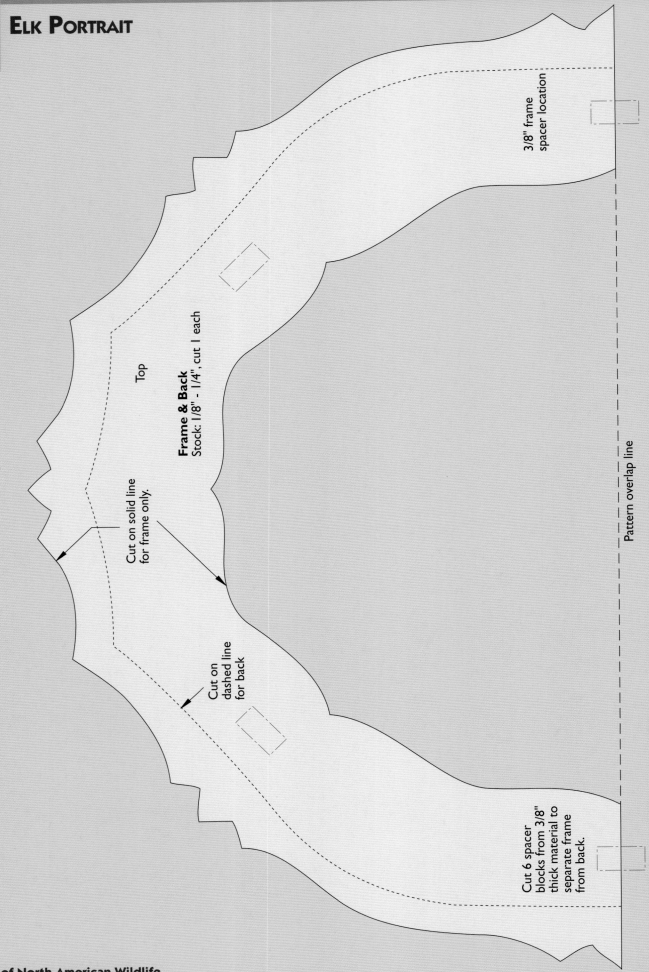

3/8" frame spacer location

Top

Frame & Back
Stock: 1/8" - 1/4", cut 1 each

Cut on solid line for frame only.

Cut on dashed line for back

Pattern overlap line

Cut 6 spacer blocks from 3/8" thick material to separate frame from back.

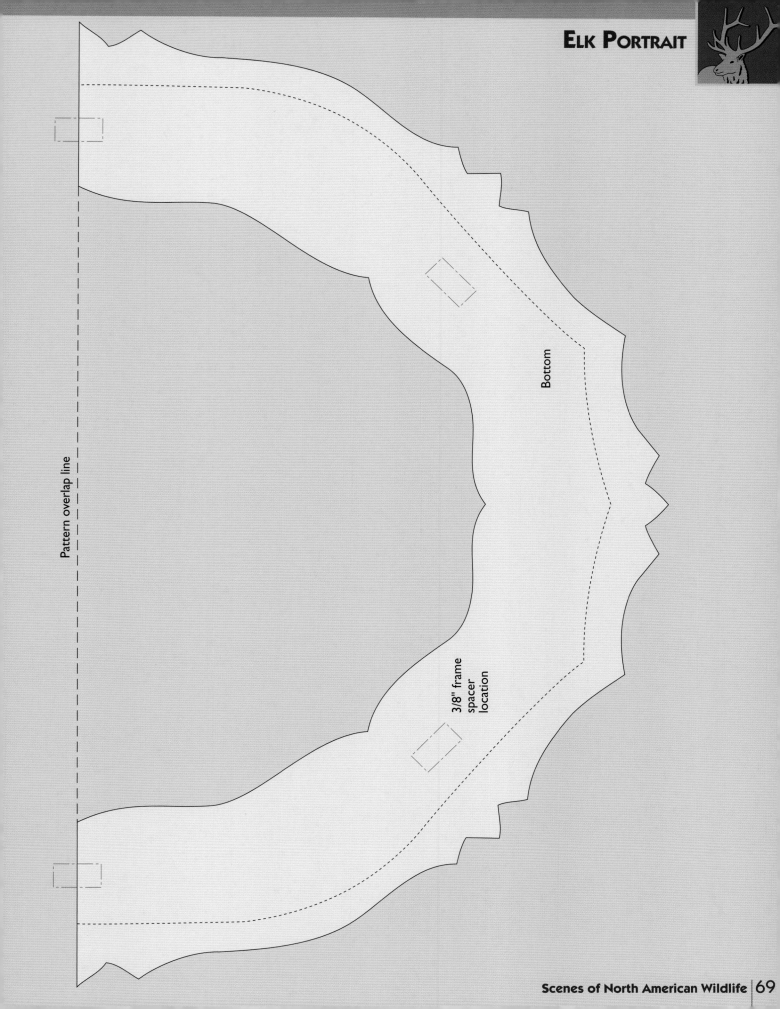

Pattern overlap line

Bottom

3/8" frame
spacer
location

ELK PORTRAIT

Mountain
Stock: 1/16" - 1/8"

Elk
Stock: 1/16" - 1/8"
Spacer: 1/4", cut 3

CARIBOU PORTRAIT

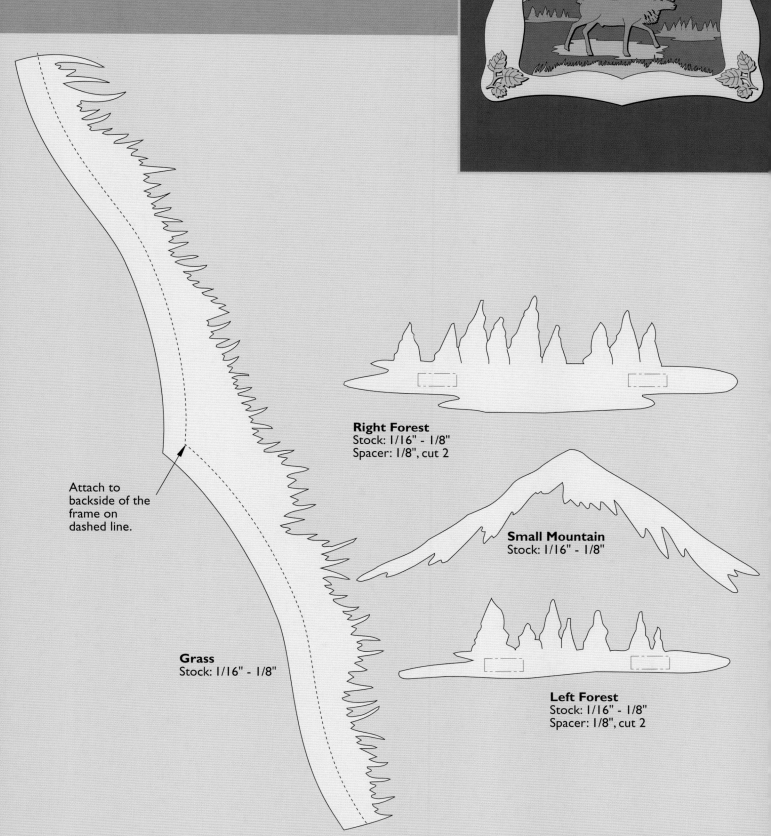

Attach to backside of the frame on dashed line.

Grass
Stock: 1/16" - 1/8"

Right Forest
Stock: 1/16" - 1/8"
Spacer: 1/8", cut 2

Small Mountain
Stock: 1/16" - 1/8"

Left Forest
Stock: 1/16" - 1/8"
Spacer: 1/8", cut 2

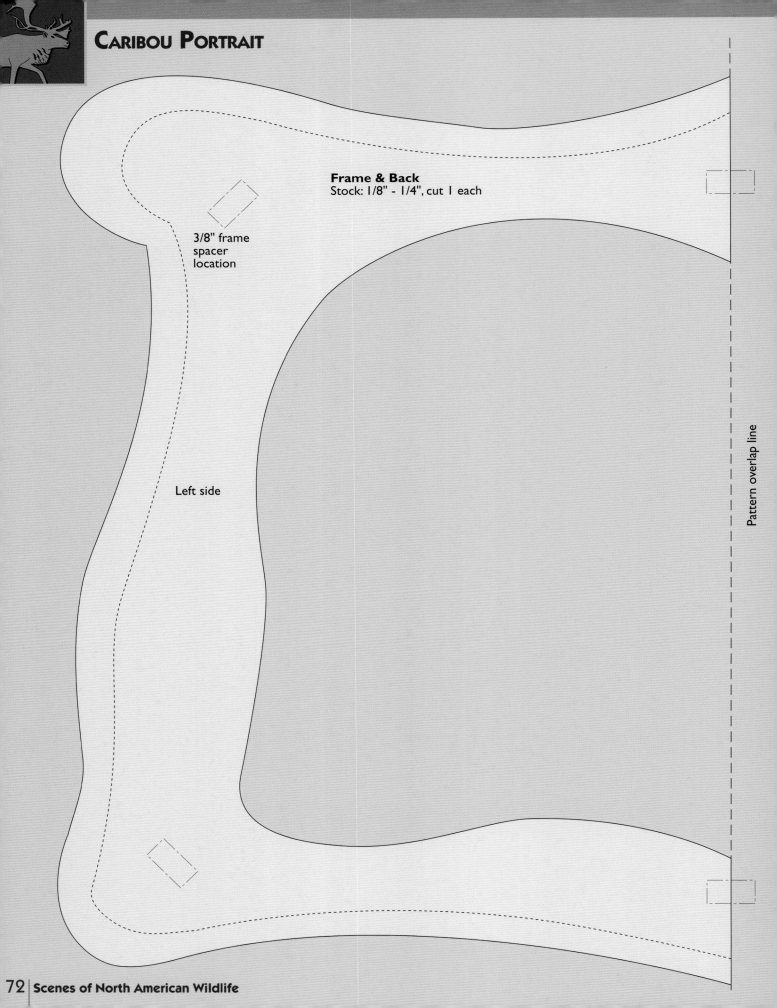

Frame & Back
Stock: 1/8" - 1/4", cut 1 each

3/8" frame
spacer
location

Left side

Pattern overlap line

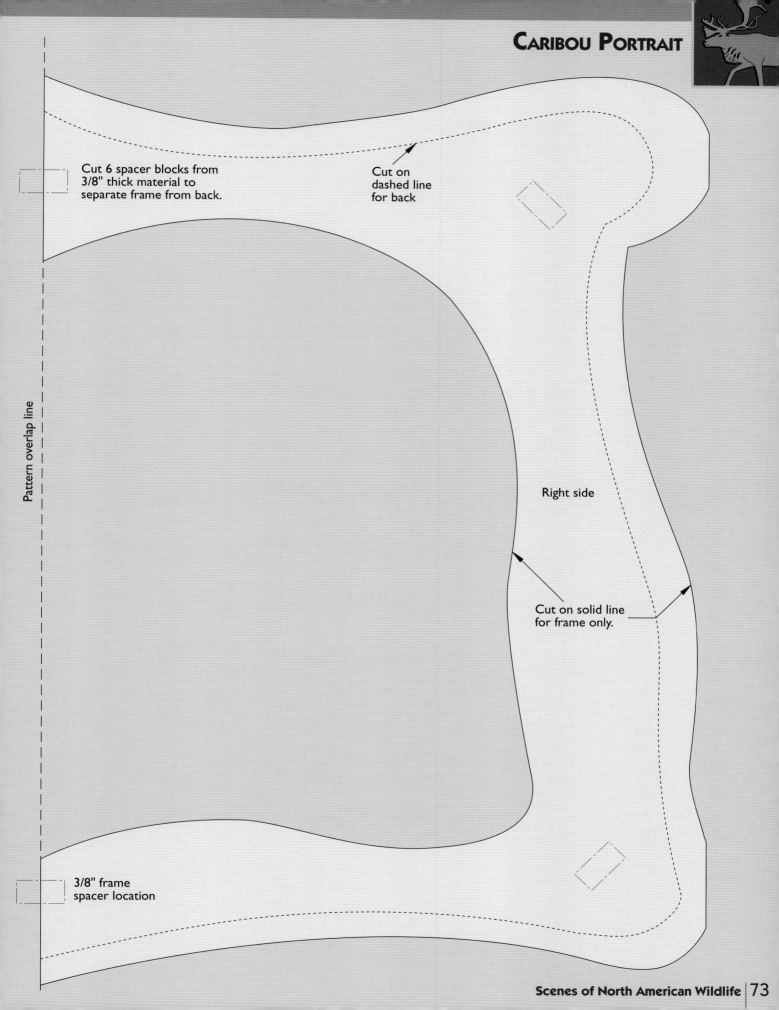

Cut 6 spacer blocks from
3/8" thick material to
separate frame from back.

Cut on
dashed line
for back

Pattern overlap line

Right side

Cut on solid line
for frame only.

3/8" frame
spacer location

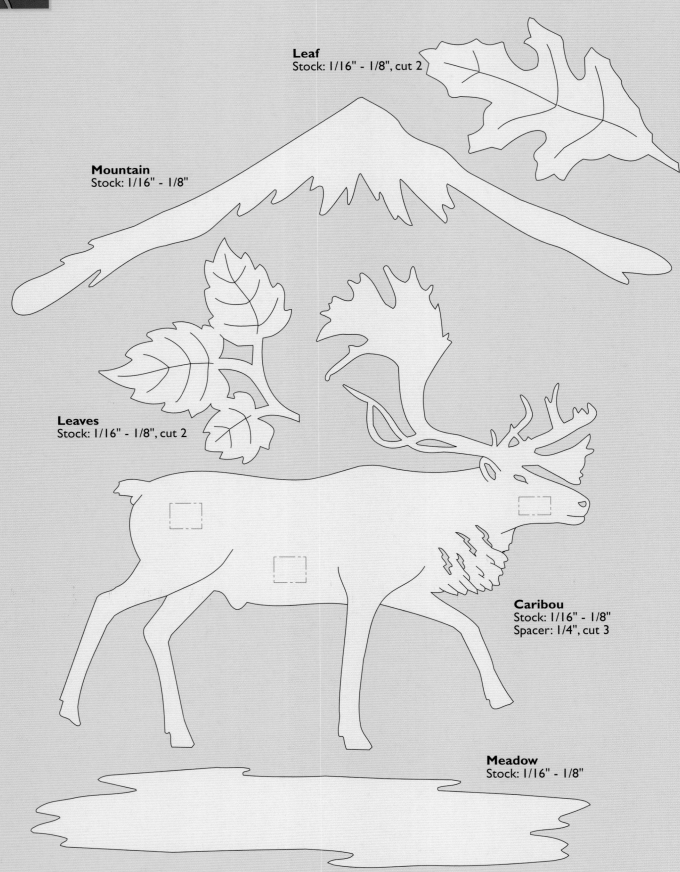

Leaf
Stock: 1/16" - 1/8", cut 2

Mountain
Stock: 1/16" - 1/8"

Leaves
Stock: 1/16" - 1/8", cut 2

Caribou
Stock: 1/16" - 1/8"
Spacer: 1/4", cut 3

Meadow
Stock: 1/16" - 1/8"

MOOSE PORTRAIT

Grass
Stock: 1/16" - 1/8"

Forest
Stock: 1/16" - 1/8"
Spacer: 1/8", cut 1

Right Trees
Stock: 1/16" - 1/8"
Spacer: 1/8", cut 2

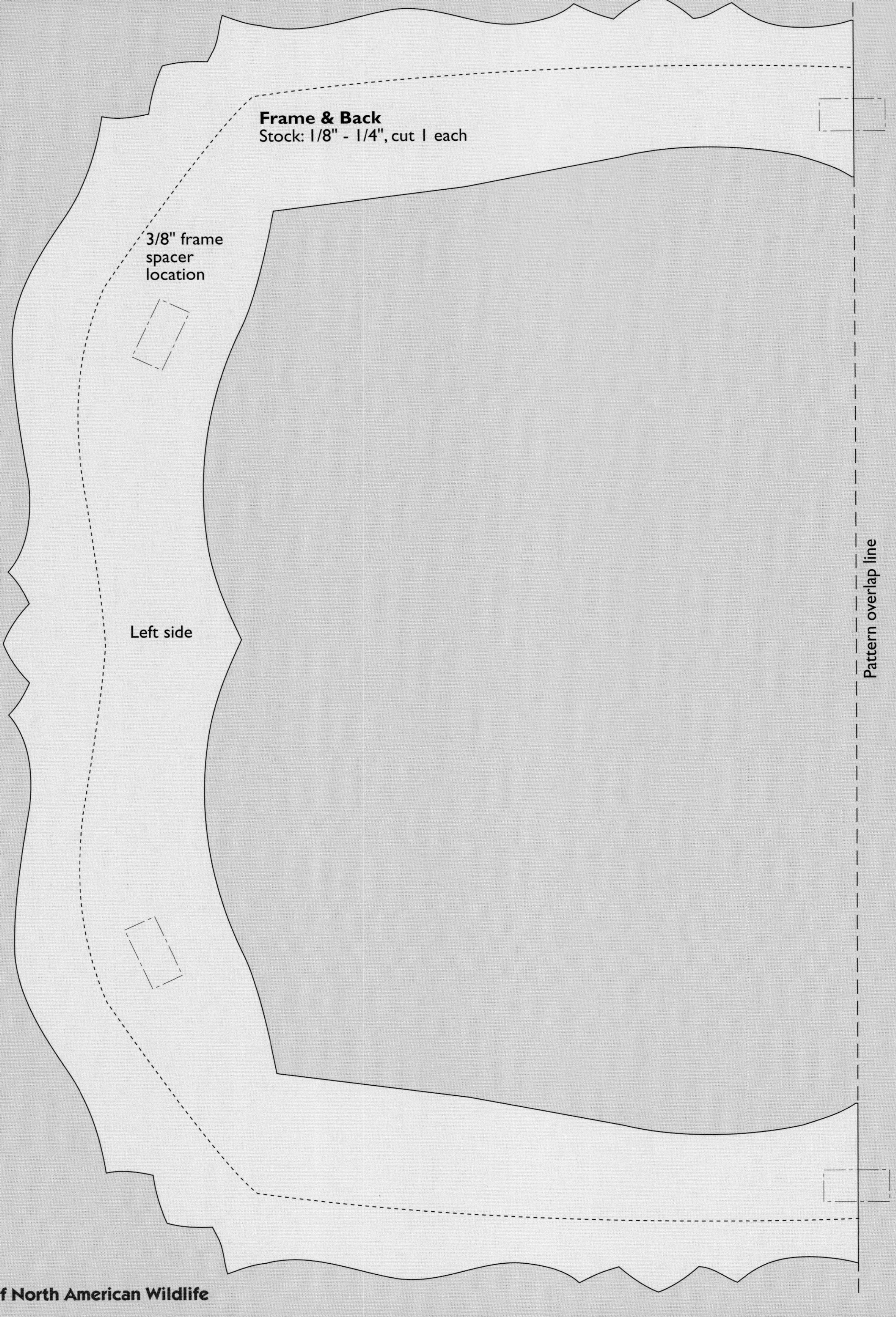

Moose Portrait

Frame & Back
Stock: 1/8" - 1/4", cut 1 each

3/8" frame
spacer
location

Left side

Pattern overlap line

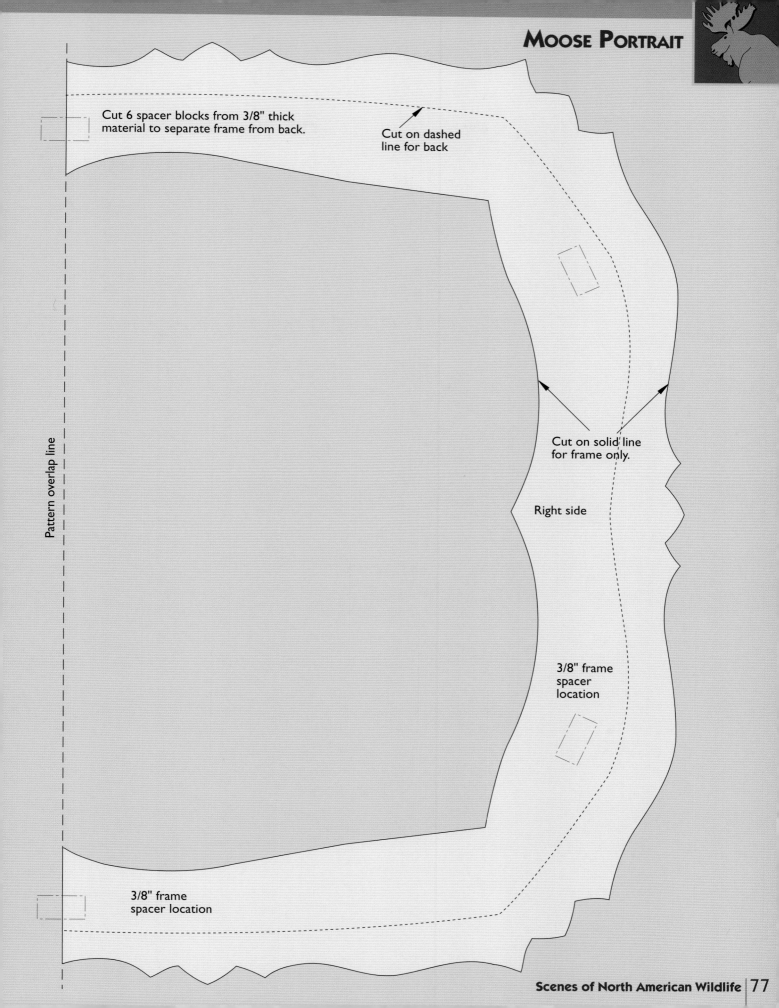

Cut 6 spacer blocks from 3/8" thick
material to separate frame from back.

Cut on dashed
line for back

Pattern overlap line

Cut on solid line
for frame only.

Right side

3/8" frame
spacer
location

3/8" frame
spacer location

MOOSE PORTRAIT

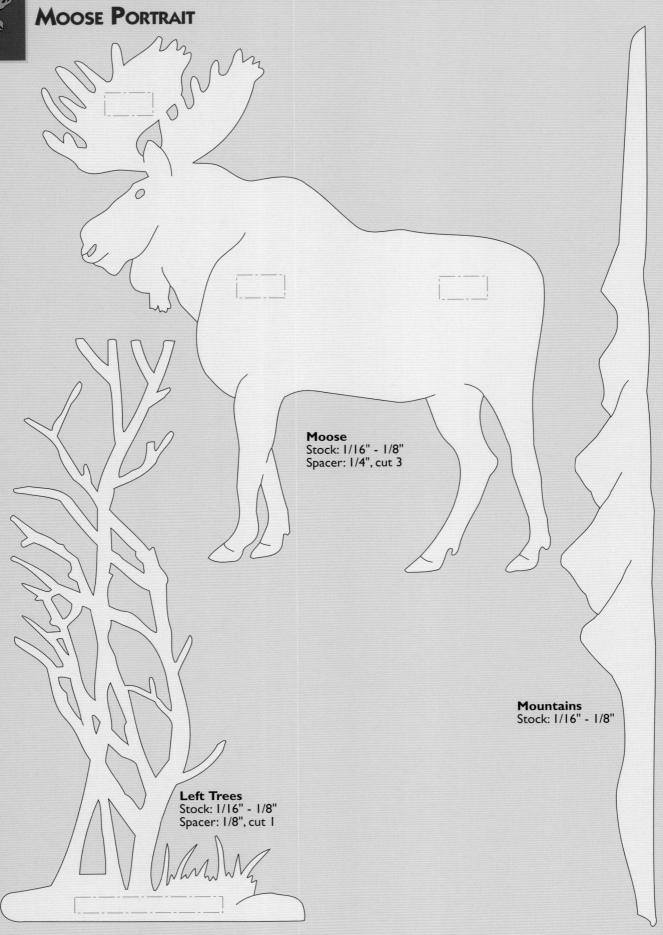

Moose
Stock: 1/16" - 1/8"
Spacer: 1/4", cut 3

Mountains
Stock: 1/16" - 1/8"

Left Trees
Stock: 1/16" - 1/8"
Spacer: 1/8", cut 1

MOUNTAIN SHEEP PAIR

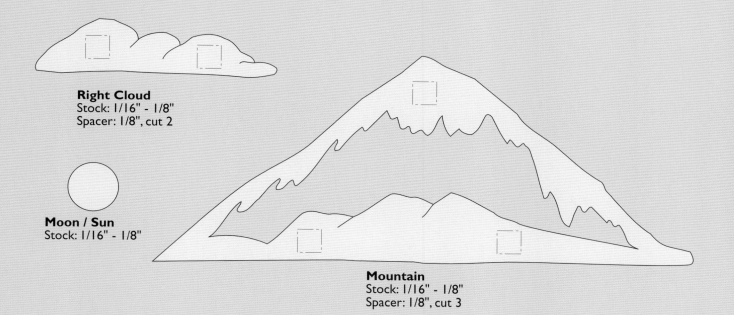

Right Cloud
Stock: 1/16" - 1/8"
Spacer: 1/8", cut 2

Moon / Sun
Stock: 1/16" - 1/8"

Mountain
Stock: 1/16" - 1/8"
Spacer: 1/8", cut 3

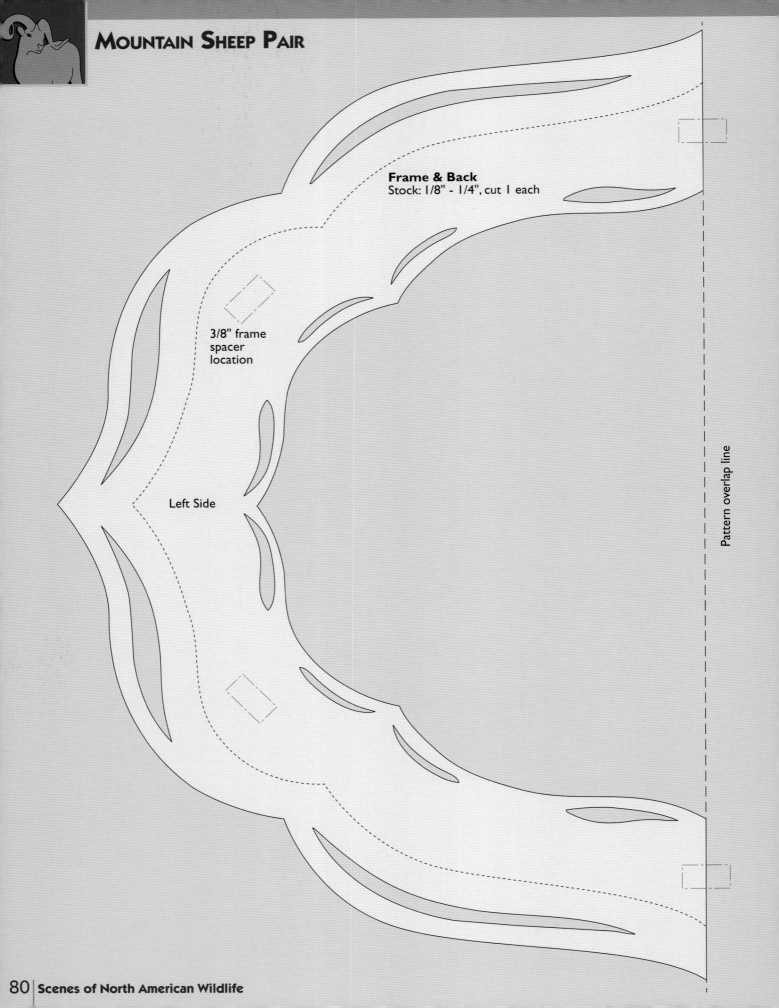

MOUNTAIN SHEEP PAIR

Frame & Back
Stock: 1/8" - 1/4", cut 1 each

3/8" frame
spacer
location

Left Side

Pattern overlap line

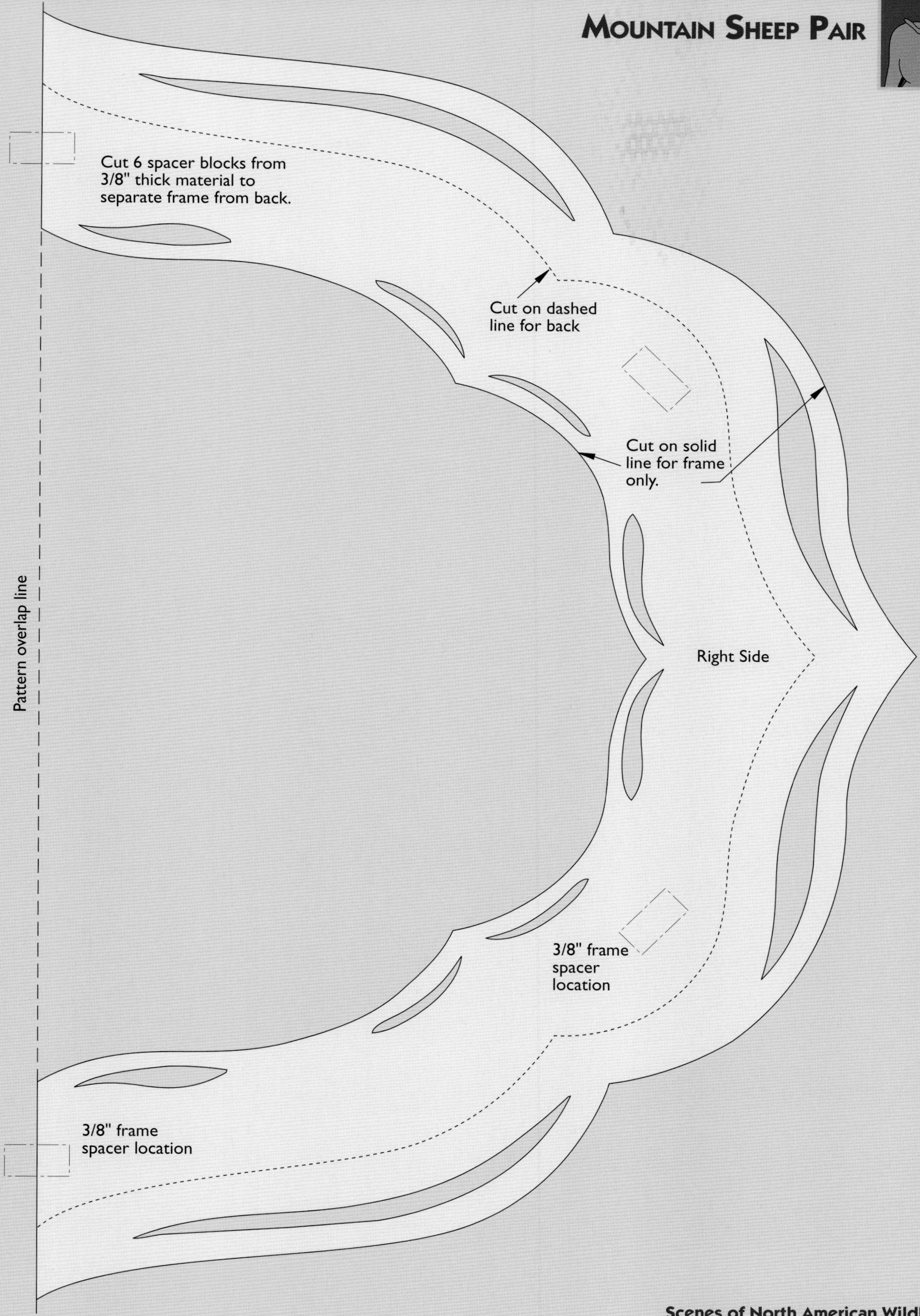

Cut 6 spacer blocks from 3/8" thick material to separate frame from back.

Cut on dashed line for back

Cut on solid line for frame only.

Right Side

Pattern overlap line

3/8" frame spacer location

3/8" frame spacer location

MOUNTAIN SHEEP PAIR

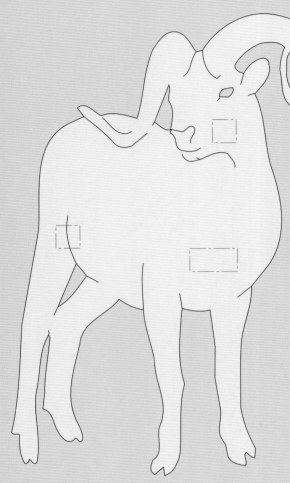

Mountain Sheep
Stock: 1/16" - 1/8"
Spacer: 3/8", cut 3

Left Cloud
Stock: 1/16" - 1/8"

Left Hills
Stock: 1/16" - 1/8"
Spacer: 1/8", cut 2

Grass
Stock: 1/16" - 1/8"
Spacer: 1/8", cut 2

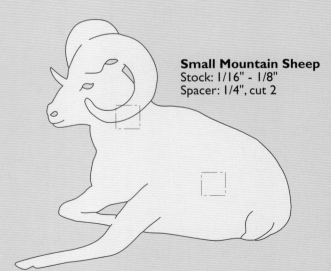

Small Mountain Sheep
Stock: 1/16" - 1/8"
Spacer: 1/4", cut 2

MOUNTAINTOP VIEW

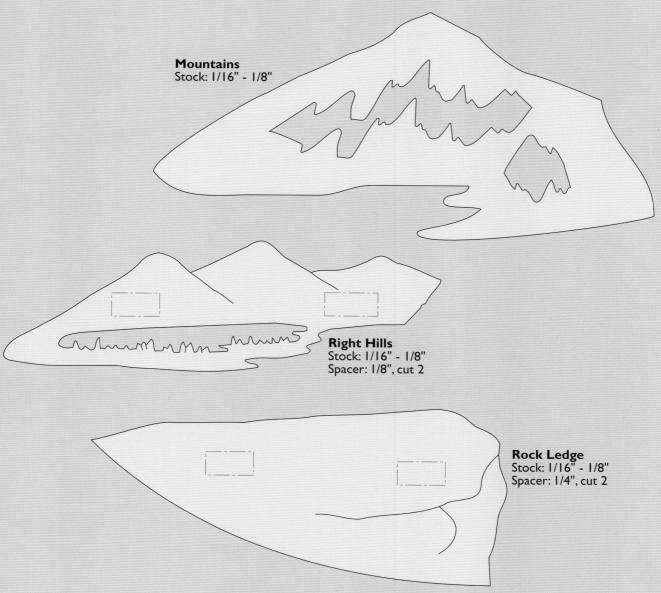

Mountains
Stock: 1/16" - 1/8"

Right Hills
Stock: 1/16" - 1/8"
Spacer: 1/8", cut 2

Rock Ledge
Stock: 1/16" - 1/8"
Spacer: 1/4", cut 2

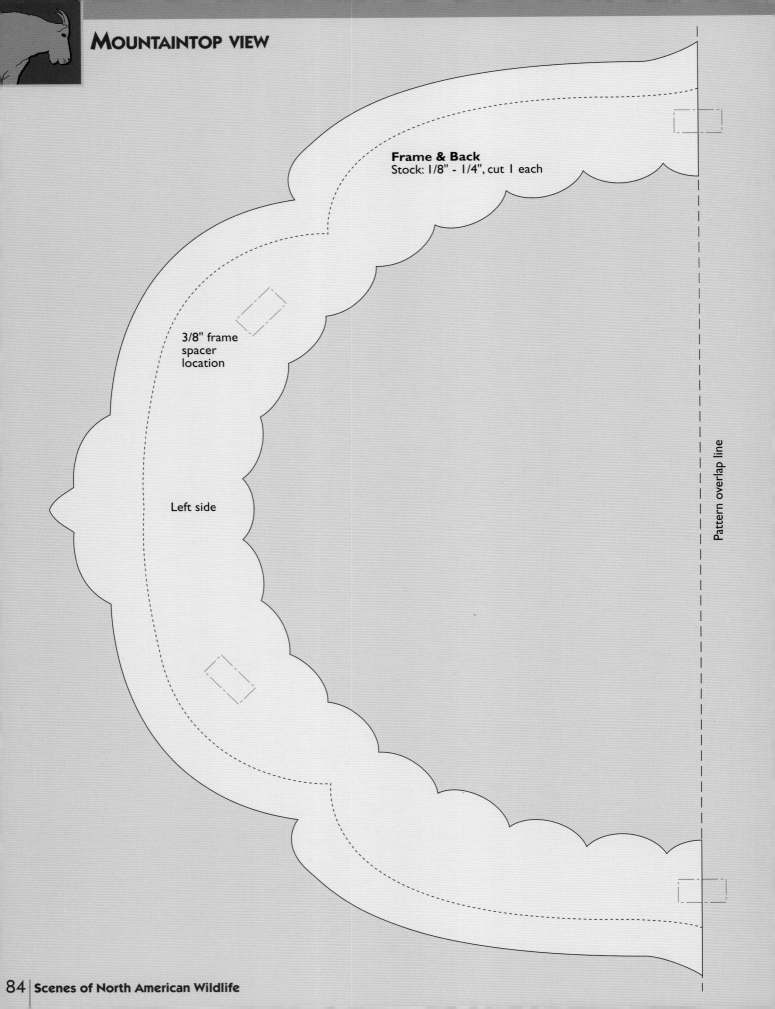

Frame & Back
Stock: 1/8" - 1/4", cut 1 each

3/8" frame
spacer
location

Left side

Pattern overlap line

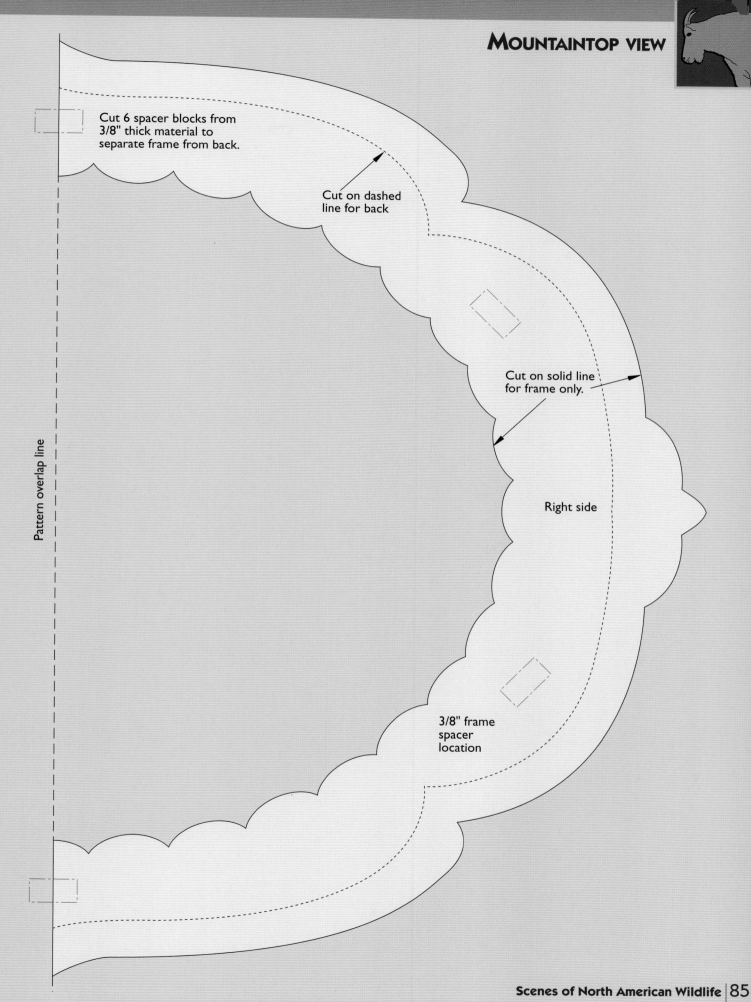

Cut 6 spacer blocks from
3/8" thick material to
separate frame from back.

Cut on dashed
line for back

Cut on solid line
for frame only.

Right side

Pattern overlap line

3/8" frame
spacer
location

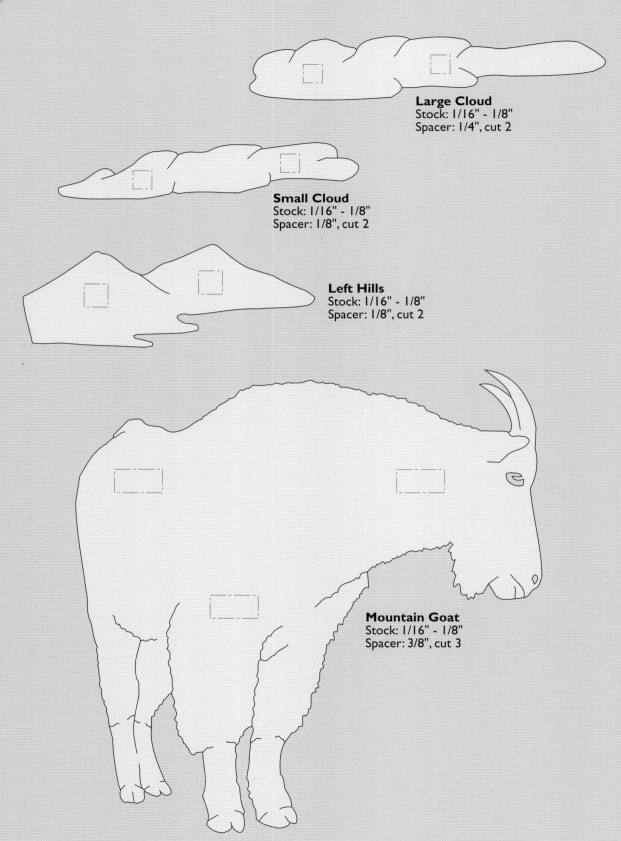

Large Cloud
Stock: 1/16" - 1/8"
Spacer: 1/4", cut 2

Small Cloud
Stock: 1/16" - 1/8"
Spacer: 1/8", cut 2

Left Hills
Stock: 1/16" - 1/8"
Spacer: 1/8", cut 2

Mountain Goat
Stock: 1/16" - 1/8"
Spacer: 3/8", cut 3

ON THE WING

Left Trees
Stock: 1/16" - 1/8"

Eagle
Stock: 1/16" - 1/8"
Spacer: 3/8", cut 3

Attach to backside
of the frame on
dashed line.

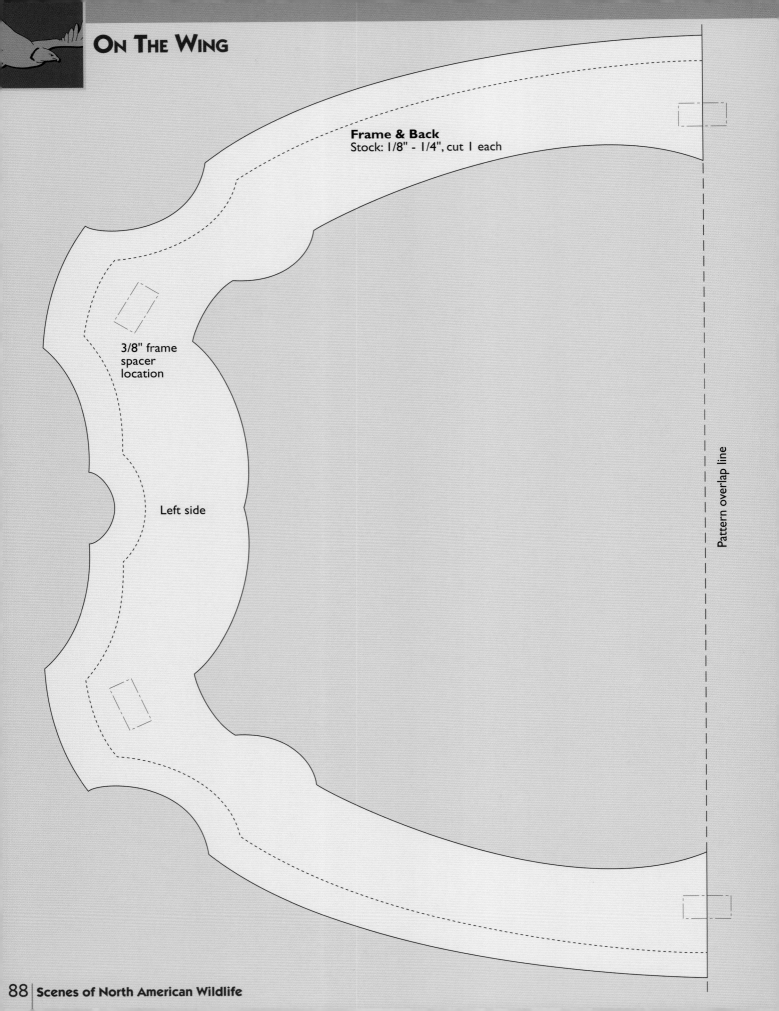

Frame & Back
Stock: 1/8" - 1/4", cut 1 each

3/8" frame
spacer
location

Left side

Pattern overlap line

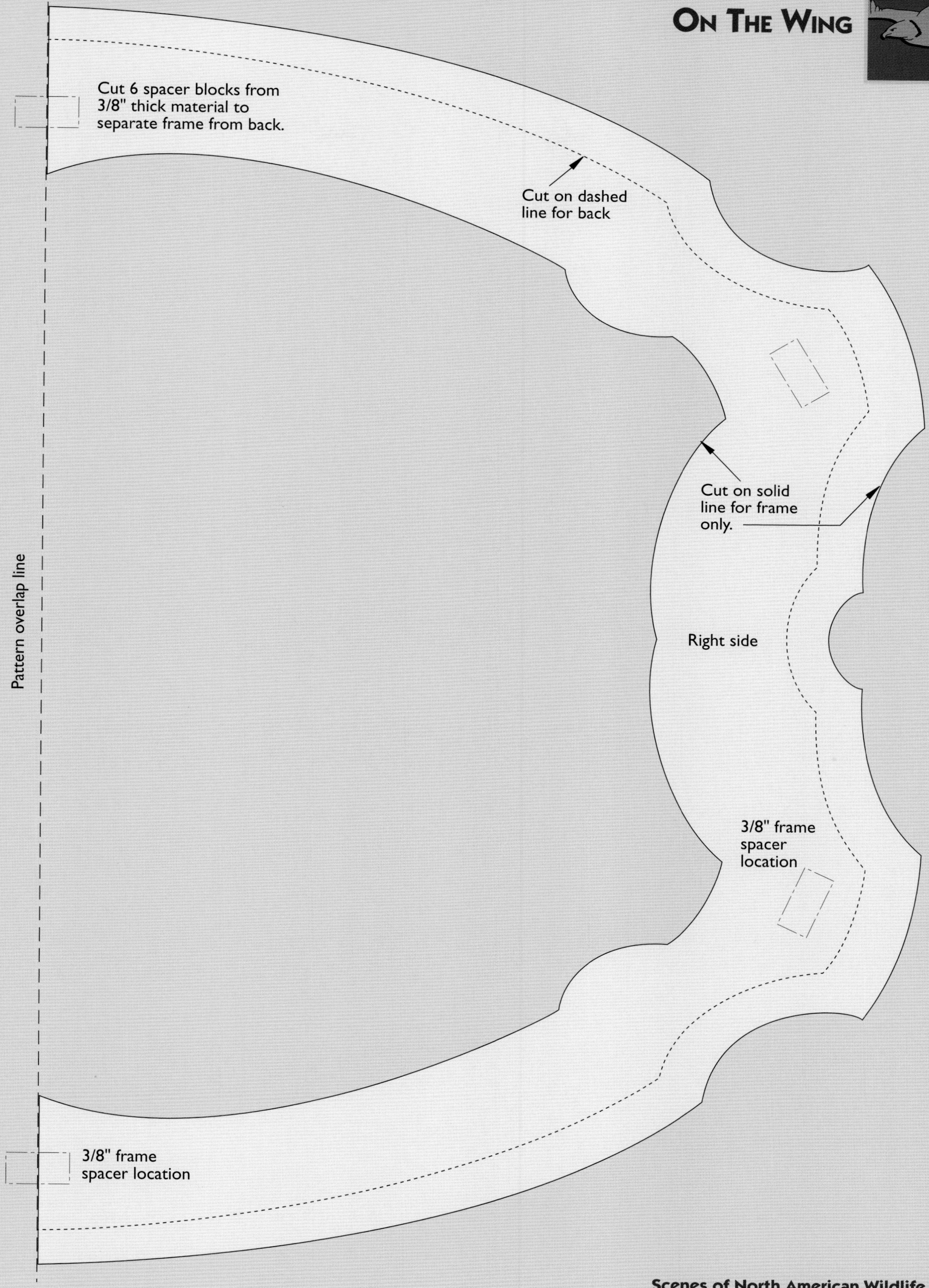

Cut 6 spacer blocks from
3/8" thick material to
separate frame from back.

Cut on dashed
line for back

Cut on solid
line for frame
only.

Right side

Pattern overlap line

3/8" frame
spacer
location

3/8" frame
spacer location

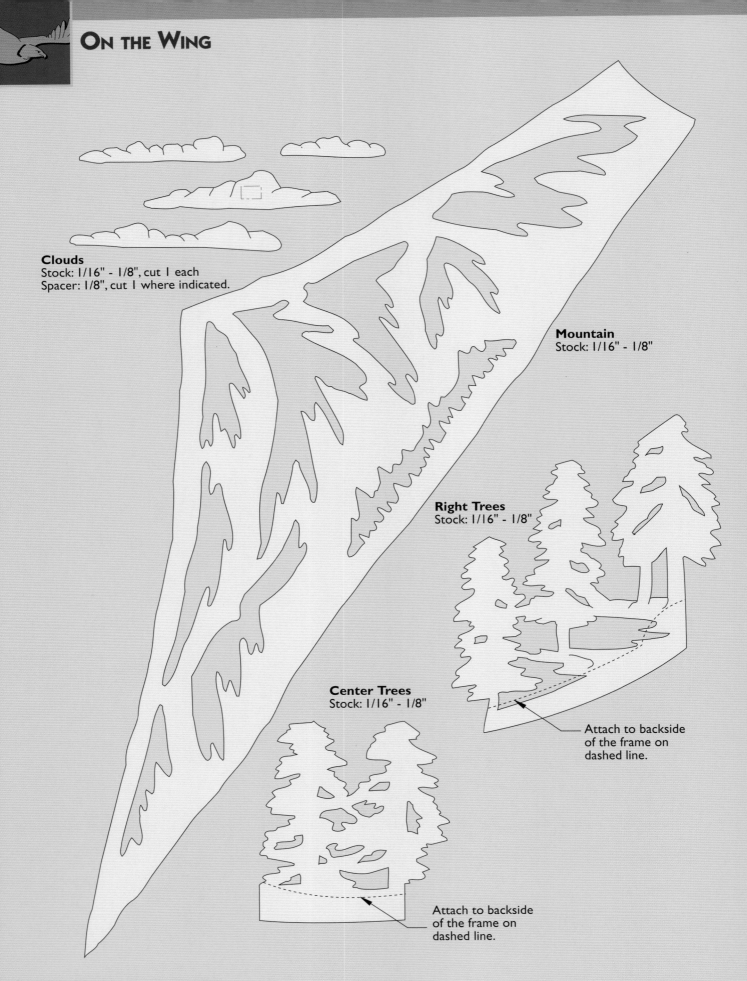

ON THE WING

Clouds
Stock: 1/16" - 1/8", cut 1 each
Spacer: 1/8", cut 1 where indicated.

Mountain
Stock: 1/16" - 1/8"

Right Trees
Stock: 1/16" - 1/8"

Attach to backside
of the frame on
dashed line.

Center Trees
Stock: 1/16" - 1/8"

Attach to backside
of the frame on
dashed line.

PREDATORY FLIGHT

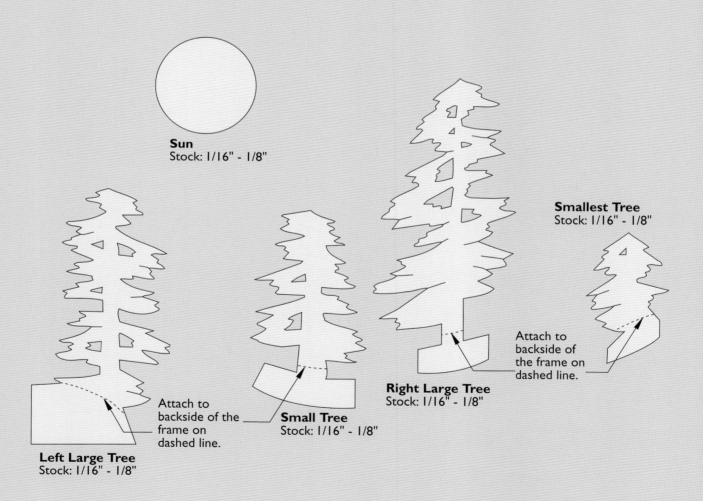

Sun
Stock: 1/16" - 1/8"

Smallest Tree
Stock: 1/16" - 1/8"

Attach to
backside of
the frame on
dashed line.

Right Large Tree
Stock: 1/16" - 1/8"

Attach to
backside of the
frame on
dashed line.

Small Tree
Stock: 1/16" - 1/8"

Attach to
backside of the
frame on
dashed line.

Left Large Tree
Stock: 1/16" - 1/8"

PREDATORY FLIGHT

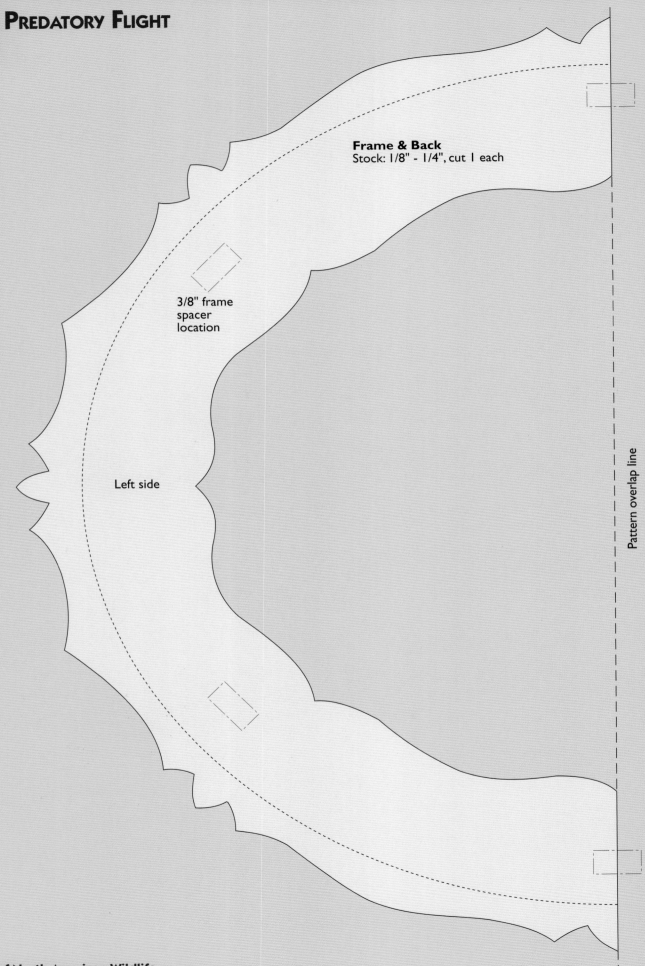

Frame & Back
Stock: 1/8" - 1/4", cut 1 each

3/8" frame
spacer
location

Left side

Pattern overlap line

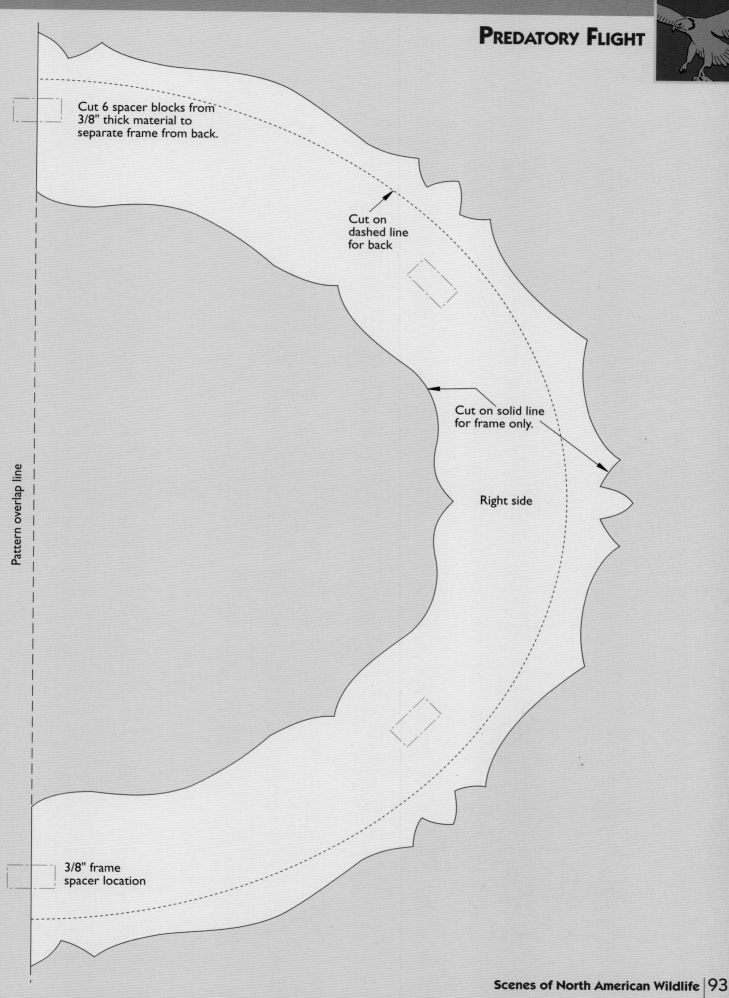

Cut 6 spacer blocks from 3/8" thick material to separate frame from back.

Cut on dashed line for back

Cut on solid line for frame only.

Right side

Pattern overlap line

3/8" frame spacer location

PREDATORY FLIGHT

Cloud
Stock: 1/16" - 1/8"
Spacer: 1/8", cut 1

Mountain
Stock: 1/16" - 1/8"
Spacer: 1/8", cut 2

Eagle
Stock: 1/16" - 1/8"
Spacer: 3/8", cut 3

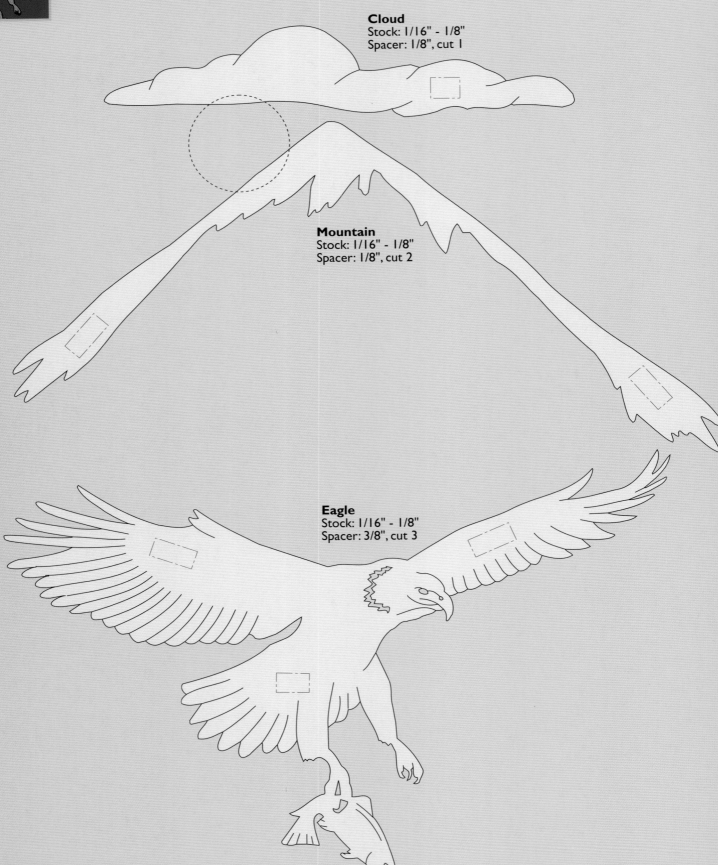

HUNTER AND HOUND

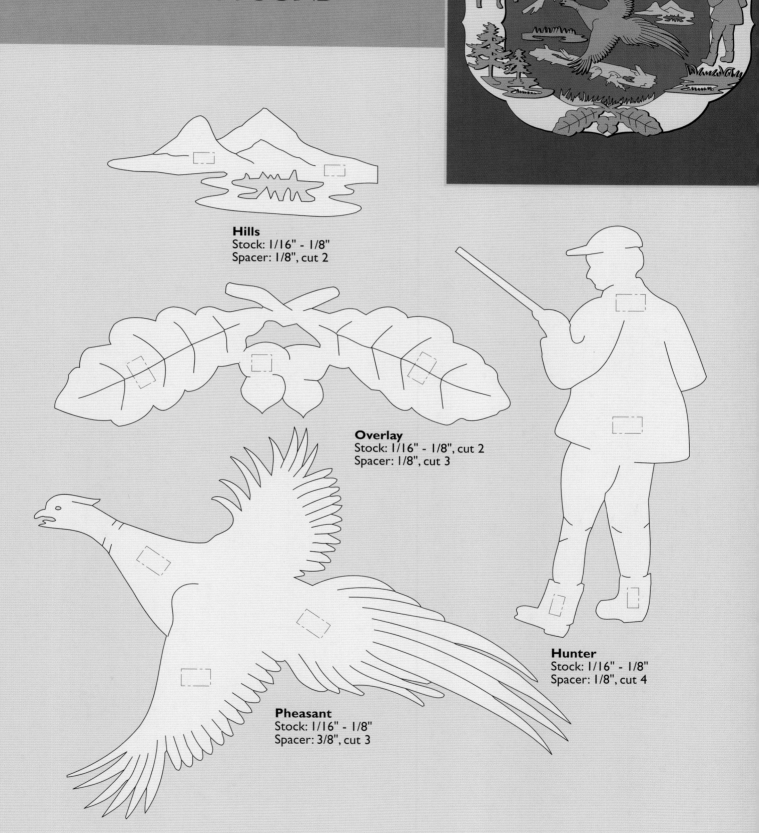

Hills
Stock: 1/16" - 1/8"
Spacer: 1/8", cut 2

Overlay
Stock: 1/16" - 1/8", cut 2
Spacer: 1/8", cut 3

Hunter
Stock: 1/16" - 1/8"
Spacer: 1/8", cut 4

Pheasant
Stock: 1/16" - 1/8"
Spacer: 3/8", cut 3

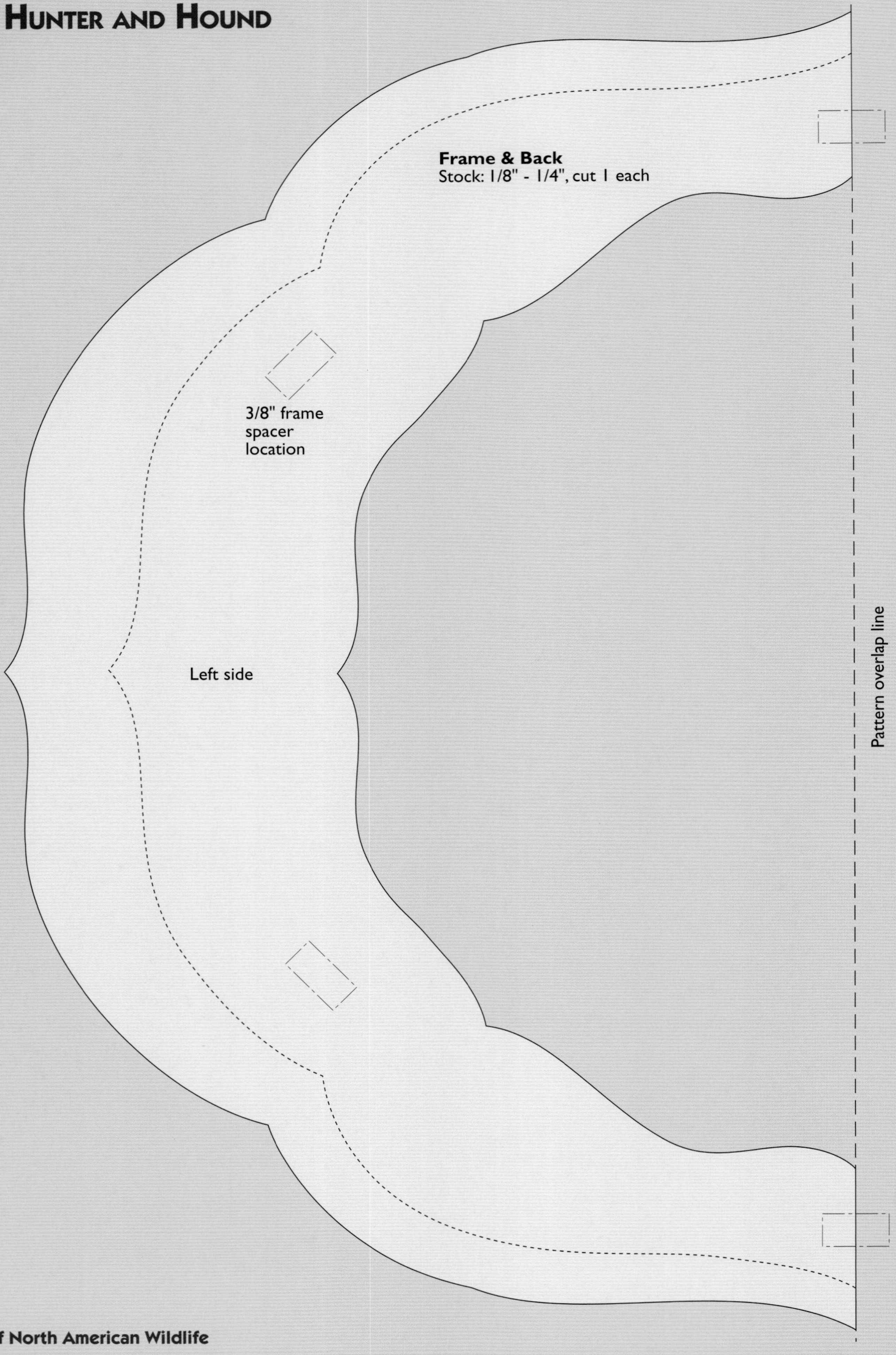

HUNTER AND HOUND

Frame & Back
Stock: 1/8" - 1/4", cut 1 each

3/8" frame
spacer
location

Left side

Pattern overlap line

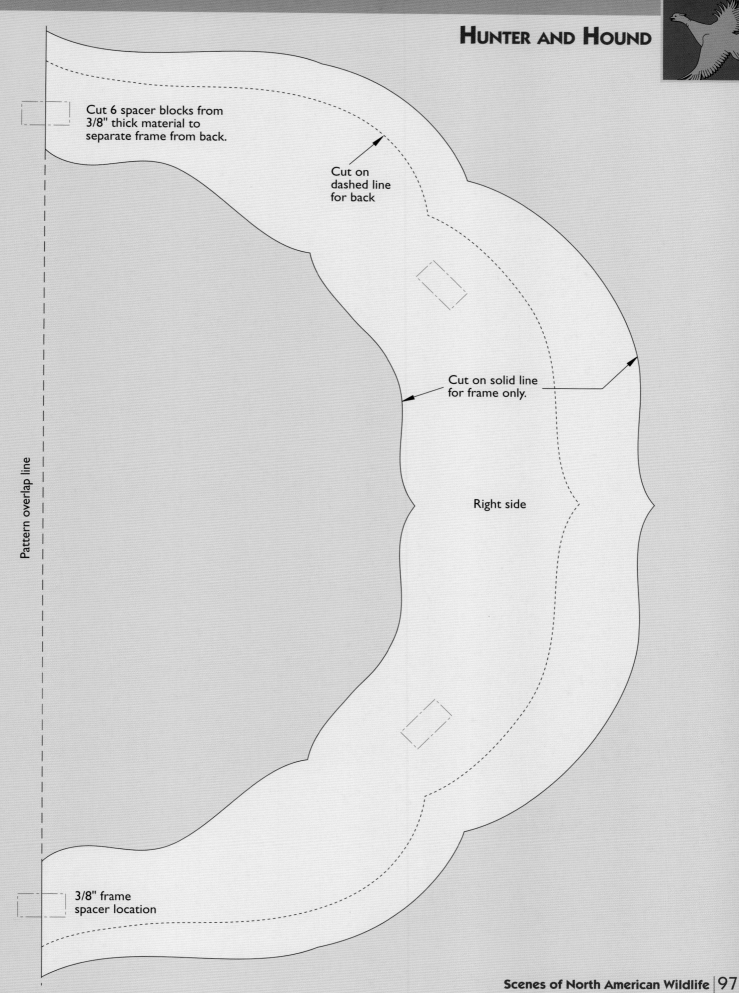

Cut 6 spacer blocks from
3/8" thick material to
separate frame from back.

Cut on
dashed line
for back

Cut on solid line
for frame only.

Pattern overlap line

Right side

3/8" frame
spacer location

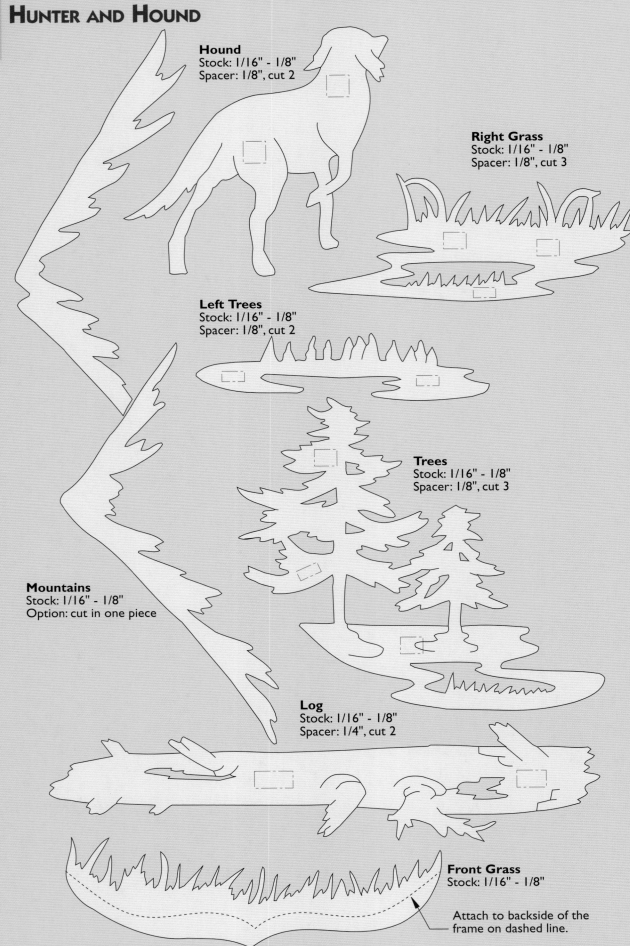

Hound
Stock: 1/16" - 1/8"
Spacer: 1/8", cut 2

Right Grass
Stock: 1/16" - 1/8"
Spacer: 1/8", cut 3

Left Trees
Stock: 1/16" - 1/8"
Spacer: 1/8", cut 2

Trees
Stock: 1/16" - 1/8"
Spacer: 1/8", cut 3

Mountains
Stock: 1/16" - 1/8"
Option: cut in one piece

Log
Stock: 1/16" - 1/8"
Spacer: 1/4", cut 2

Front Grass
Stock: 1/16" - 1/8"

Attach to backside of the
frame on dashed line.

DUCK IN FLIGHT

Right Mountains
Stock: 1/16" - 1/8"

Forest
Stock: 1/16" - 1/8"
Spacer: 1/8", cut 2

Clouds
Stock: 1/16" - 1/8", cut 1 each
Spacer: 1/8", cut 2 where indicated.

Duck
Stock: 1/16" - 1/8"
Spacer: 1/2", cut 3

Tree
Stock: 1/16" - 1/8"
Spacer: 1/8", cut 3

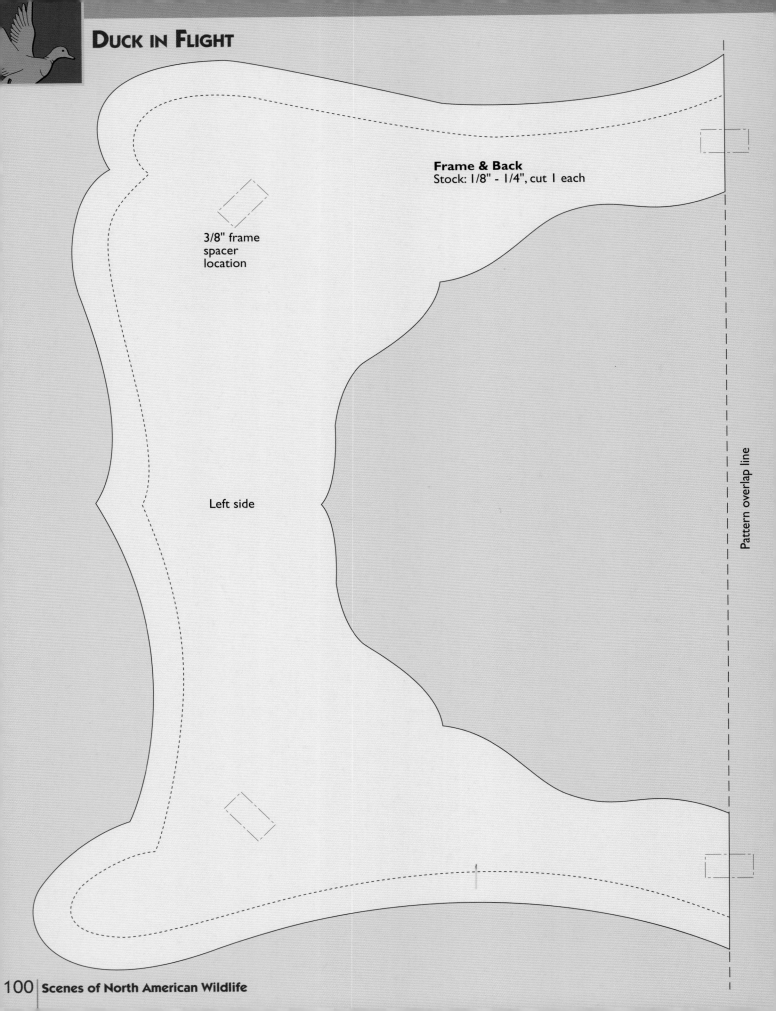

Duck in Flight

Frame & Back
Stock: 1/8" - 1/4", cut 1 each

3/8" frame
spacer
location

Left side

Pattern overlap line

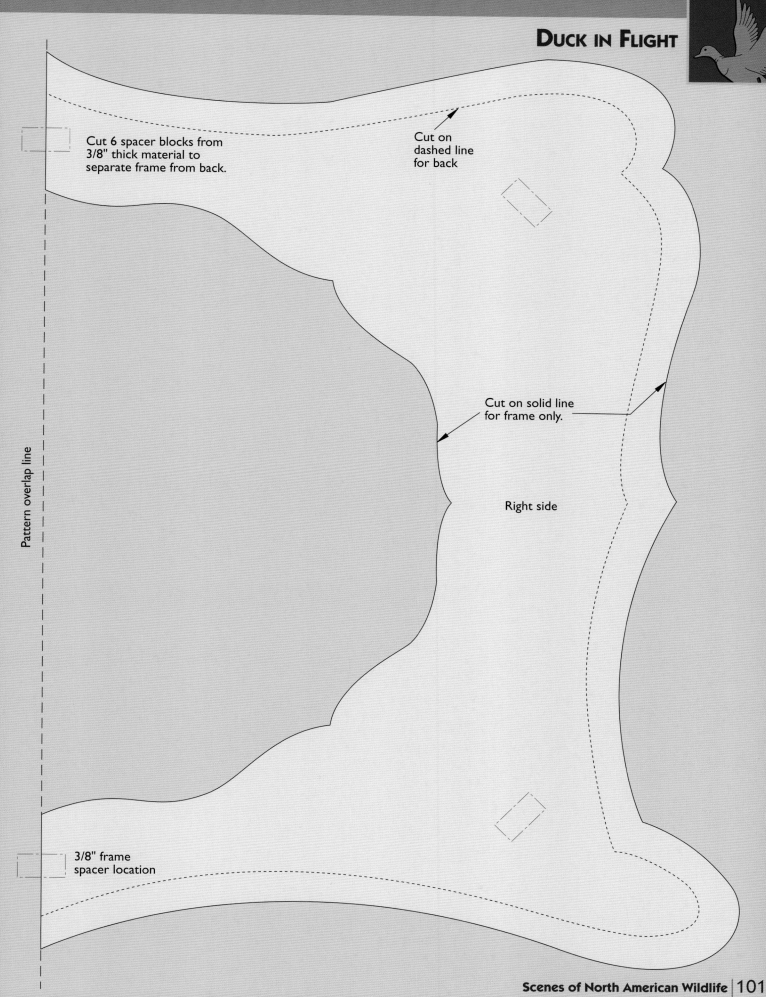

Cut 6 spacer blocks from
3/8" thick material to
separate frame from back.

Cut on
dashed line
for back

Cut on solid line
for frame only.

Right side

Pattern overlap line

3/8" frame
spacer location

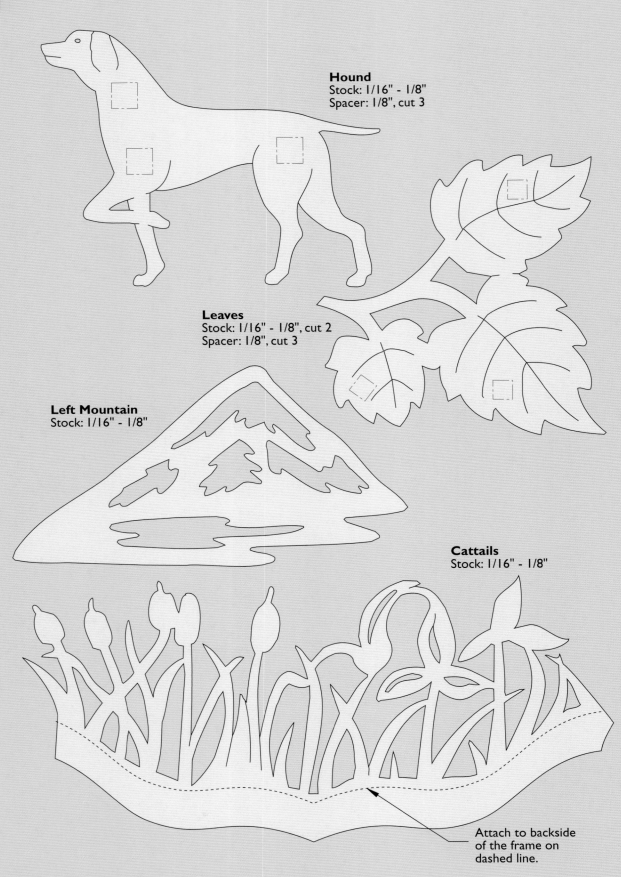

Hound
Stock: 1/16" - 1/8"
Spacer: 1/8", cut 3

Leaves
Stock: 1/16" - 1/8", cut 2
Spacer: 1/8", cut 3

Left Mountain
Stock: 1/16" - 1/8"

Cattails
Stock: 1/16" - 1/8"

Attach to backside
of the frame on
dashed line.

DUCK PAIR

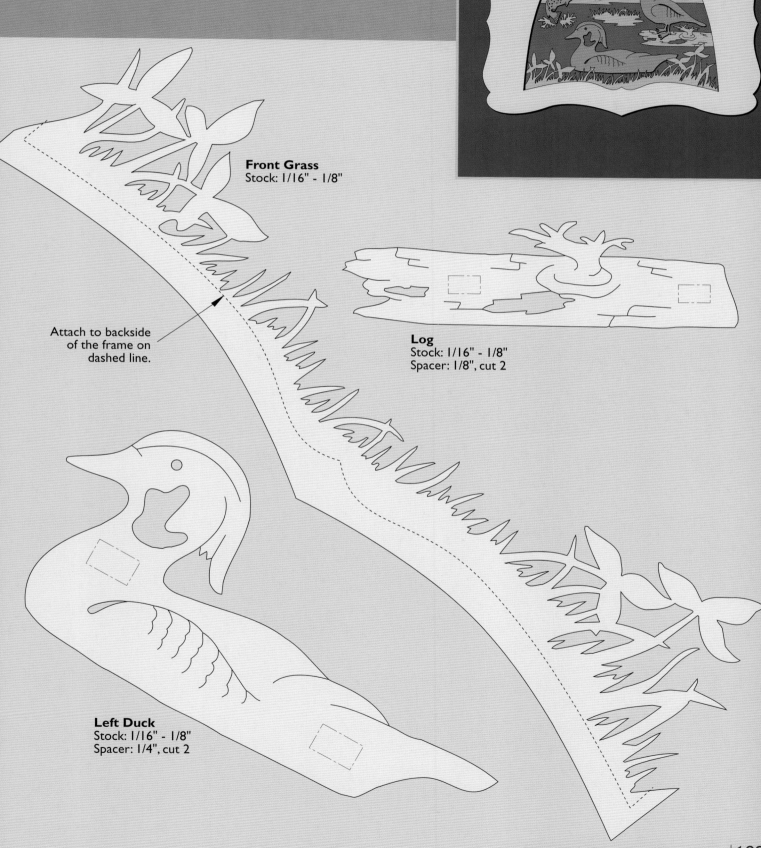

Front Grass
Stock: 1/16" - 1/8"

Attach to backside
of the frame on
dashed line.

Log
Stock: 1/16" - 1/8"
Spacer: 1/8", cut 2

Left Duck
Stock: 1/16" - 1/8"
Spacer: 1/4", cut 2

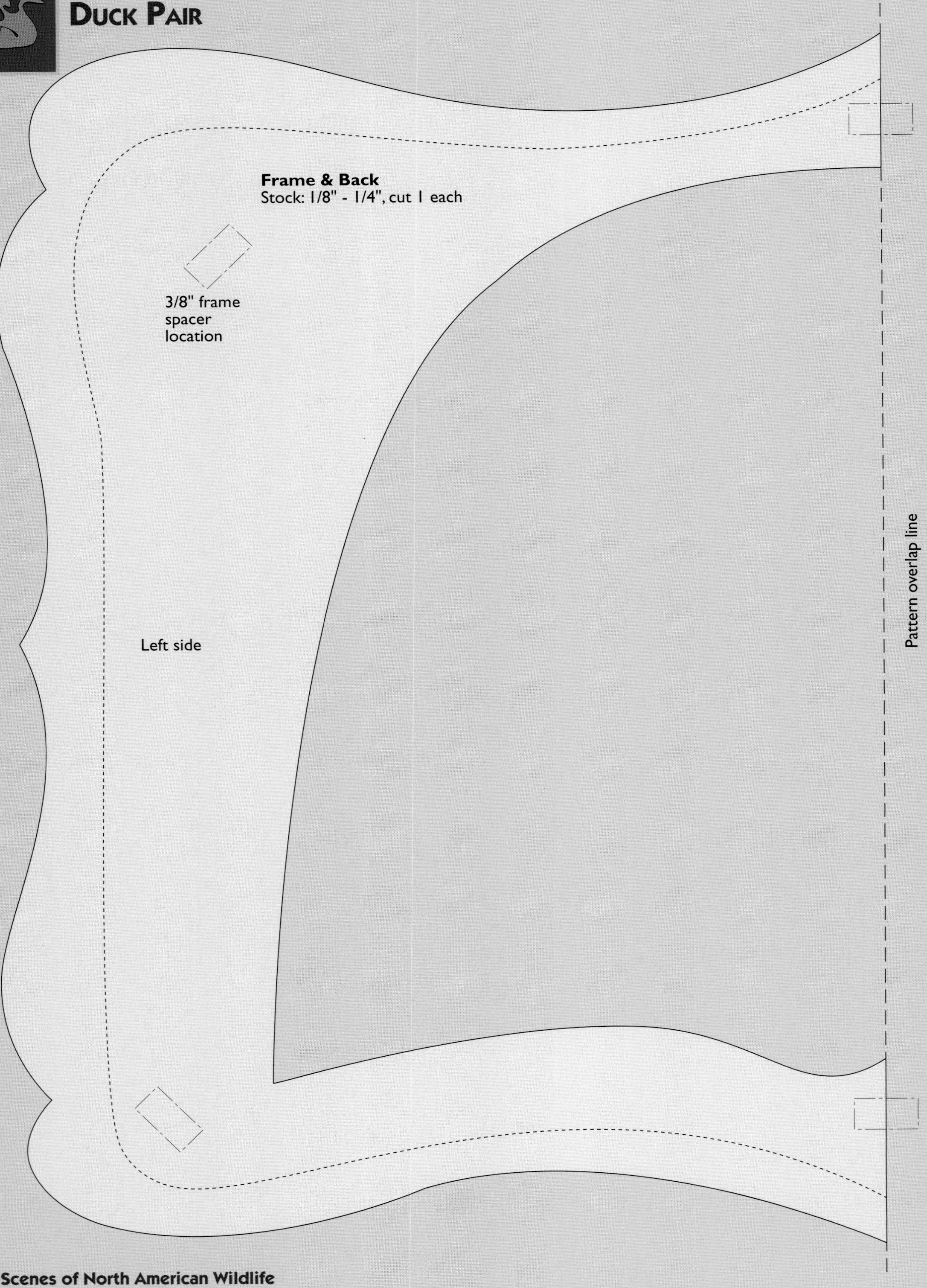

Frame & Back
Stock: 1/8" - 1/4", cut 1 each

3/8" frame
spacer
location

Left side

Pattern overlap line

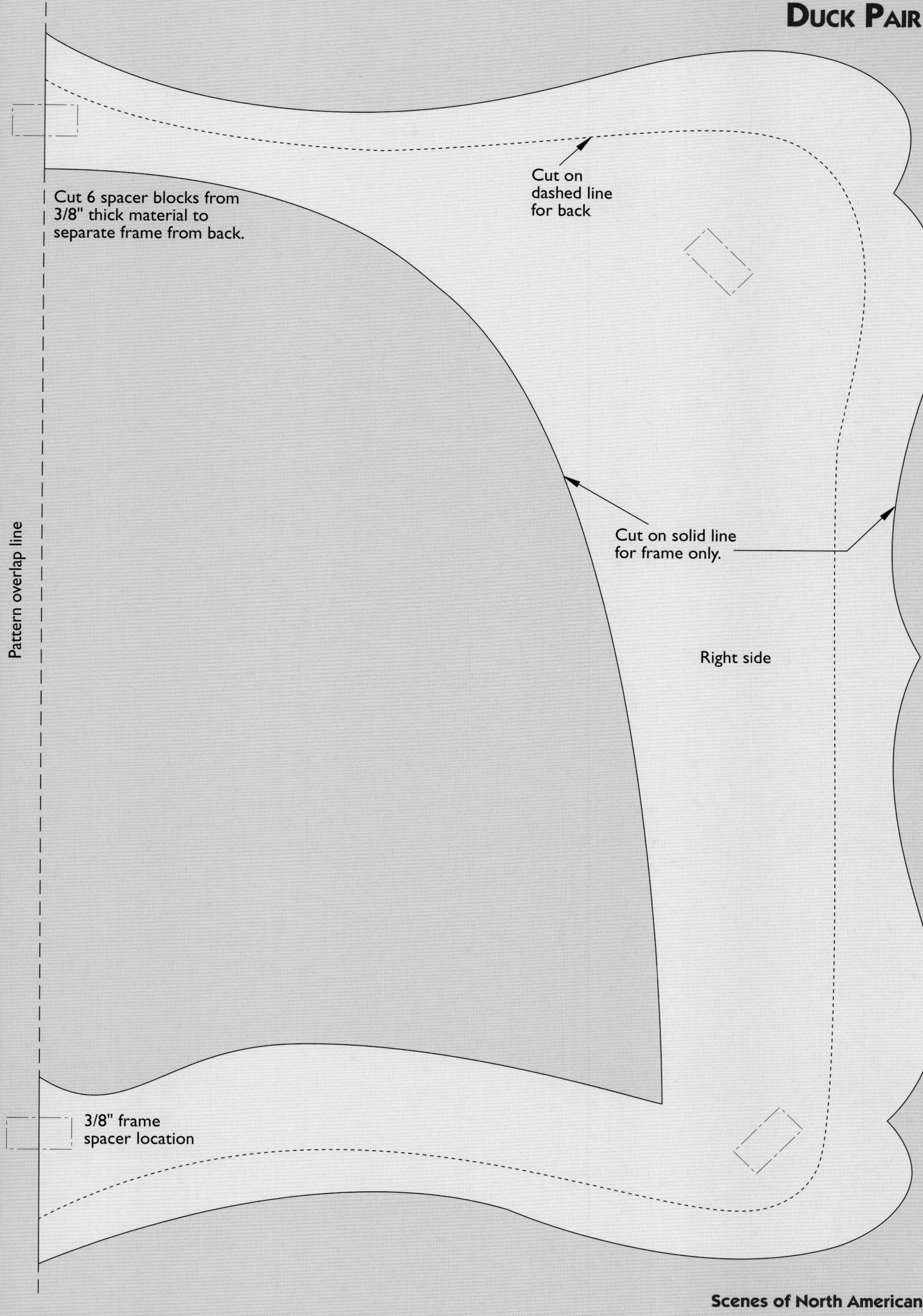

DUCK PAIR

Cut on
dashed line
for back

Cut 6 spacer blocks from
3/8" thick material to
separate frame from back.

Pattern overlap line

Cut on solid line
for frame only.

Right side

3/8" frame
spacer location

DUCK PAIR

Small Cloud
Stock: 1/16" - 1/8"

Large Cloud
Stock: 1/16" - 1/8"
Spacer: 1/8", cut 2

Overlay
Stock: 1/16" - 1/8", cut 2

Hills
Stock: 1/16" - 1/8"

Back Grass
Stock: 1/16" - 1/8"
Spacer: 1/8", cut 2

Fish
Stock: 1/16" - 1/8"
Spacer: 1/8", cut 1

Water
Stock: 1/16" - 1/8"

Right Duck
Stock: 1/16" - 1/8"
Spacer: 1/4", cut 3

HERON PORTRAIT

Heron
Stock: 1/16" - 1/8"
Spacer: 3/8", cut 3

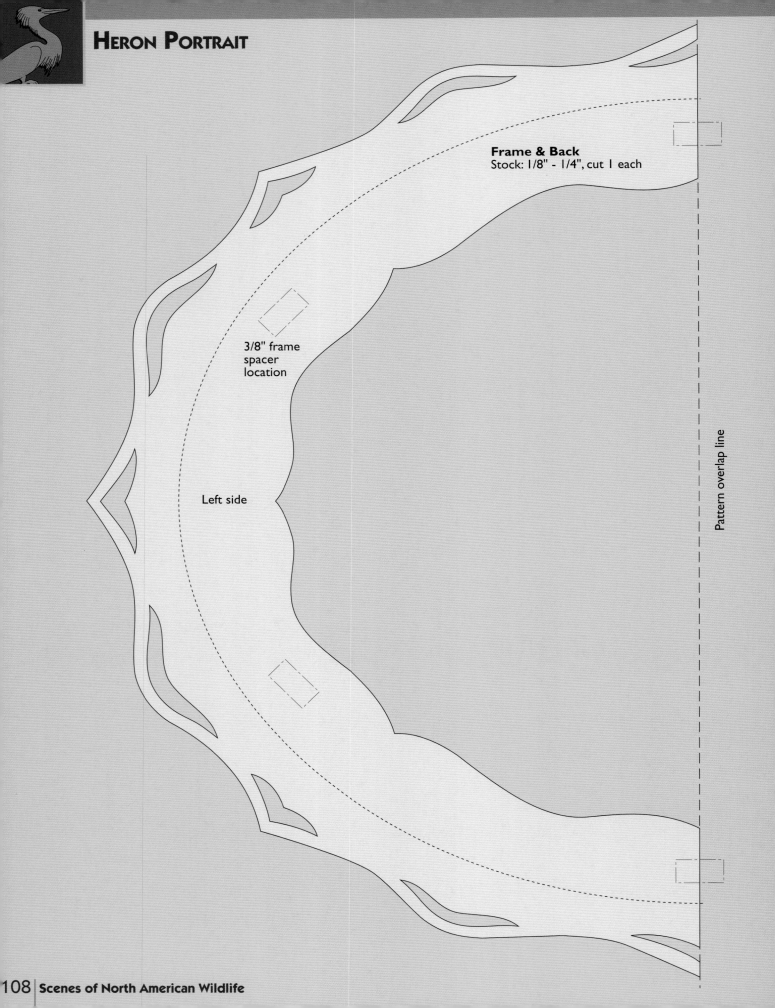

HERON PORTRAIT

Frame & Back
Stock: 1/8" - 1/4", cut 1 each

3/8" frame
spacer
location

Left side

Pattern overlap line

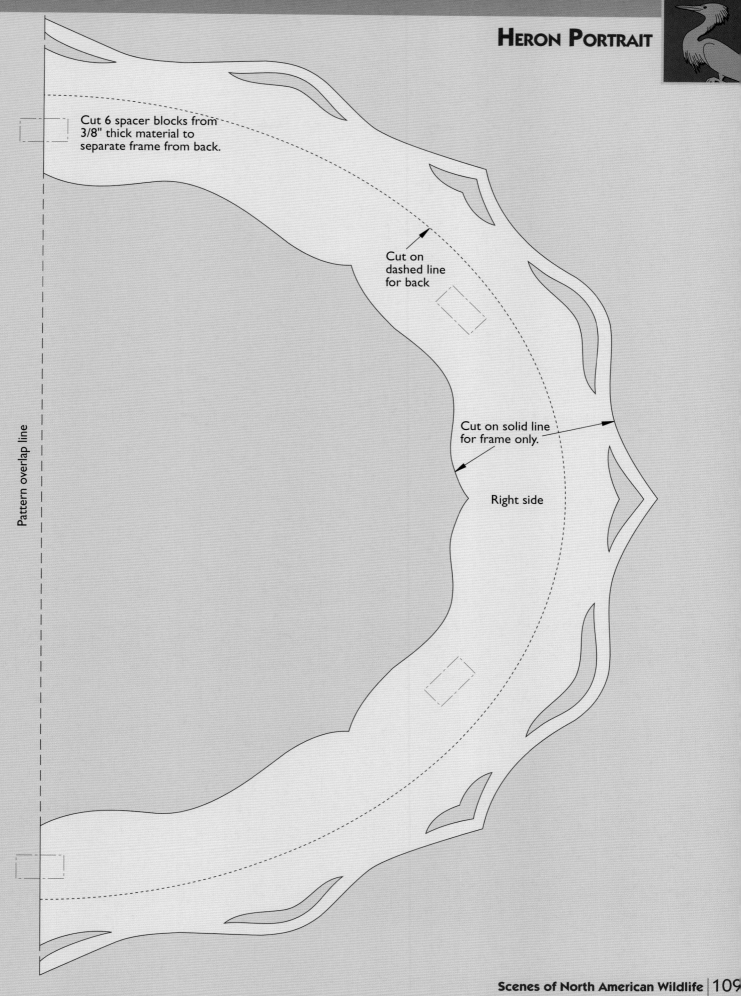

Cut 6 spacer blocks from 3/8" thick material to separate frame from back.

Cut on dashed line for back

Cut on solid line for frame only.

Right side

Pattern overlap line

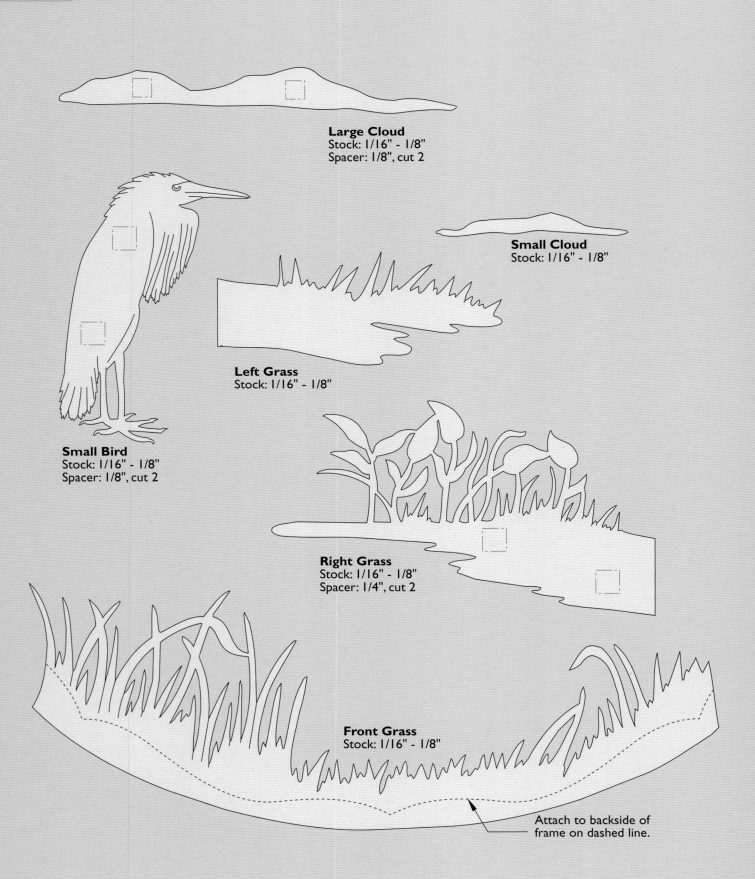

Large Cloud
Stock: 1/16" - 1/8"
Spacer: 1/8", cut 2

Small Cloud
Stock: 1/16" - 1/8"

Left Grass
Stock: 1/16" - 1/8"

Small Bird
Stock: 1/16" - 1/8"
Spacer: 1/8", cut 2

Right Grass
Stock: 1/16" - 1/8"
Spacer: 1/4", cut 2

Front Grass
Stock: 1/16" - 1/8"

Attach to backside of
frame on dashed line.

SWAN LAKE

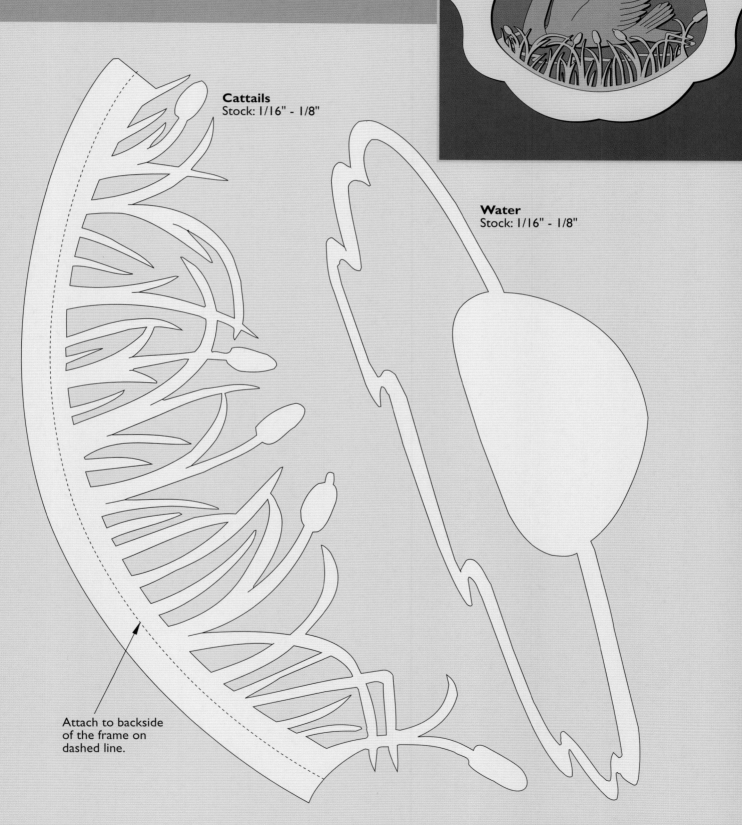

Cattails
Stock: 1/16" - 1/8"

Water
Stock: 1/16" - 1/8"

Attach to backside
of the frame on
dashed line.

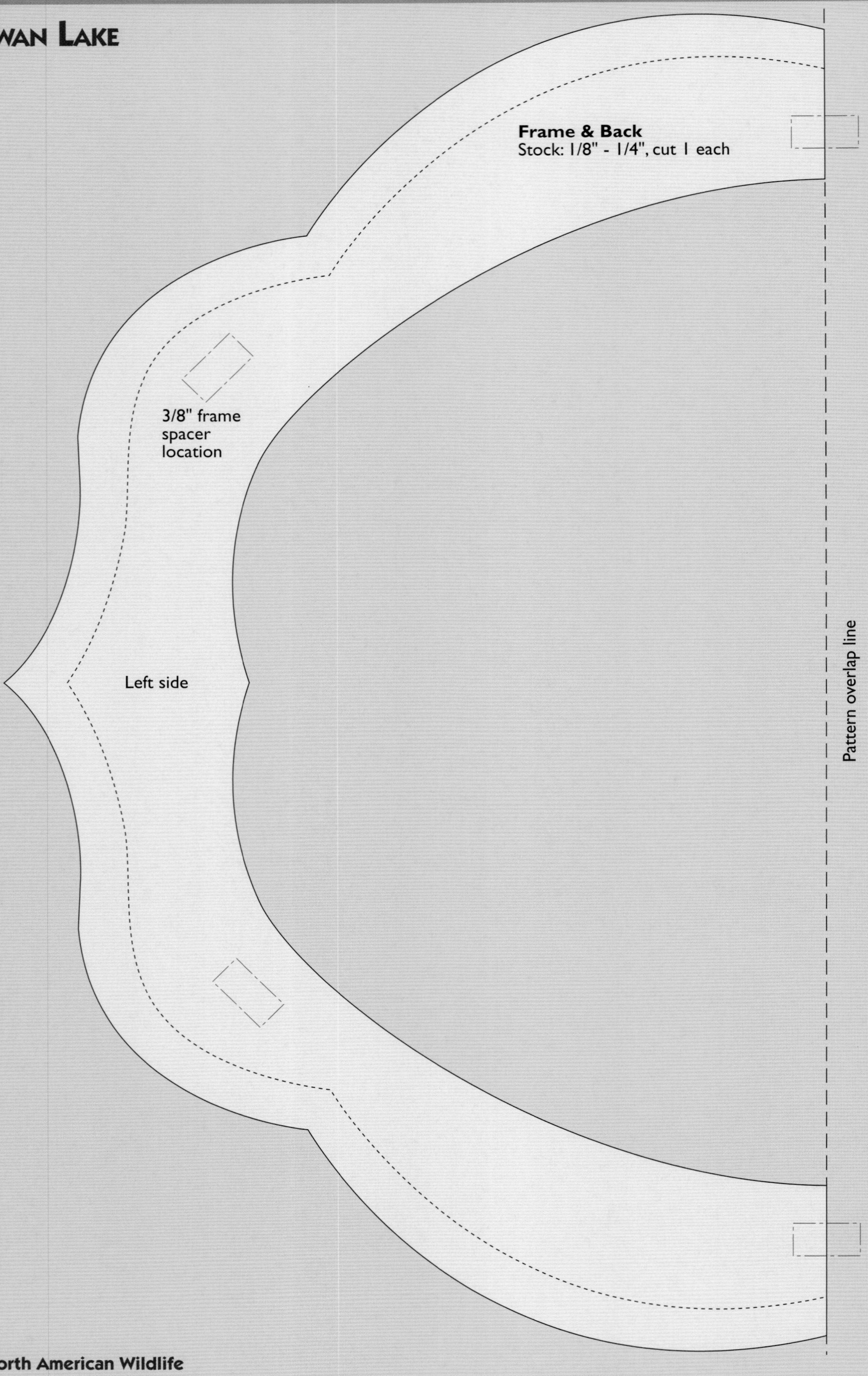

Frame & Back
Stock: 1/8" - 1/4", cut 1 each

3/8" frame
spacer
location

Left side

Pattern overlap line

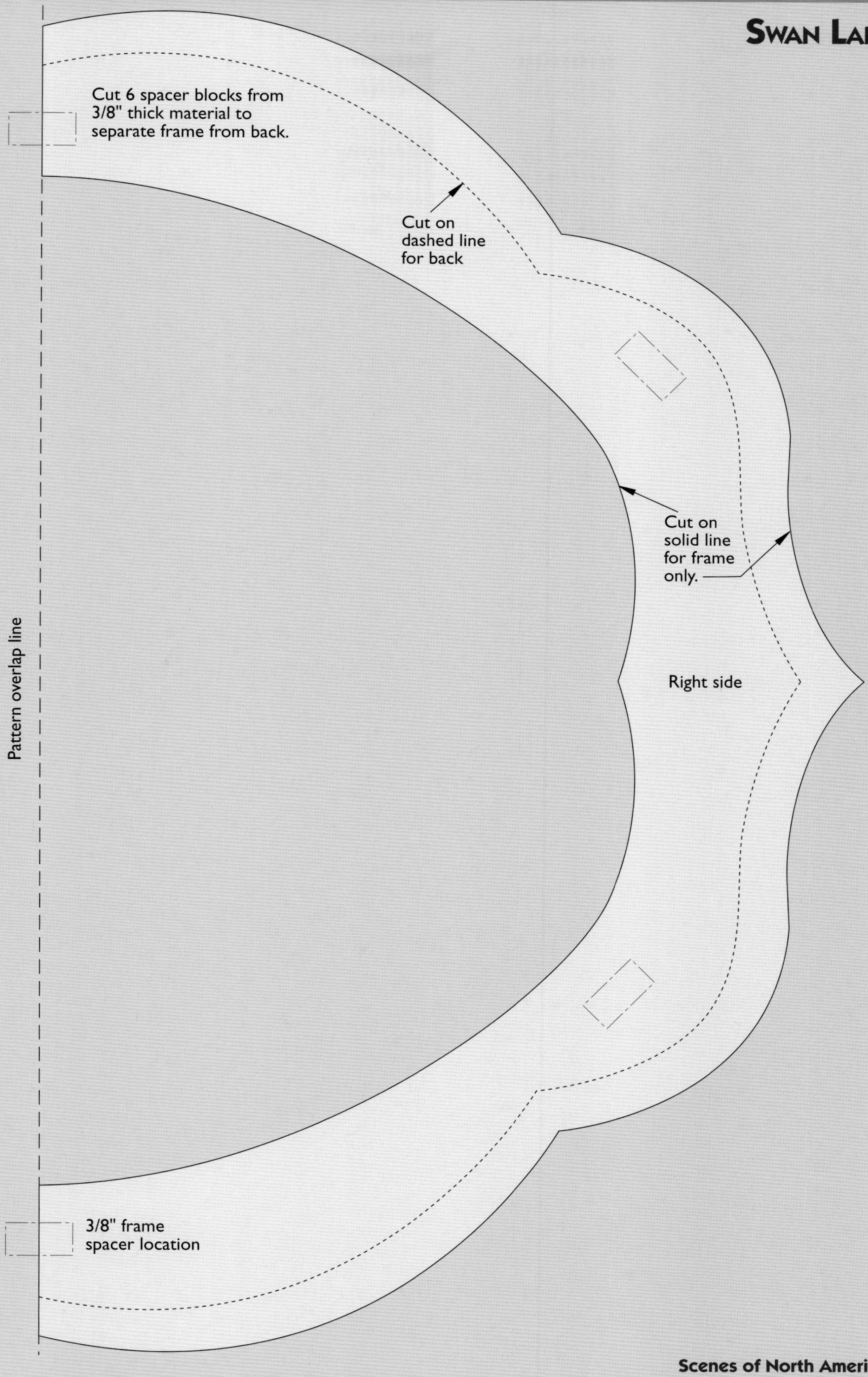

Cut 6 spacer blocks from
3/8" thick material to
separate frame from back.

Cut on
dashed line
for back

Cut on
solid line
for frame
only.

Right side

Pattern overlap line

3/8" frame
spacer location

Center Mountain
Stock: 1/16" - 1/8"

Left Mountain
Stock: 1/16" - 1/8"

Swan
Stock: 1/16" - 1/8"
Spacer: 1/8", cut 3

Right Mountain
Stock: 1/16" - 1/8"

Left Cloud
Stock: 1/16" - 1/8"
Spacer: 1/8", cut 1

Right Cloud
Stock: 1/16" - 1/8"

All of the frames and figures are designed to be interchangeable with each other so that you can customize your wildlife scenes. The following index lists the elements of all of the projects in this book so that you can easily find the pieces you need to create your own custom projects.

RESOURCES

To find materials and supplies for scroll sawing, contact The Berry Basket, PO Box 925, Centralia, WA 98531, 1–800–206–9009, **www.berrybasket.com**.

More Great Project Books from Fox Chapel Publishing

Miniature Clocks for the Scroll Saw
Over 250 Patterns from The Berry Basket Collection
by Rick and Karen Longabaugh
Price: $16.95
Soft Cover
ISBN: 1-56523-275-5
Pages 128
8.5" x 11"

Holiday Ornaments for the Scroll Saw
Over 300 Beautiful Patterns from The Berry Basket Collection
by Rick and Karen Longabaugh
Price: $16.95
Soft Cover
ISBN: 1-56523-276-3
Pages 120
8.5" x 11"

Animal Puzzles for the Scroll Saw
by Judy and Dave Peterson
Price: $14.95
Soft Cover
ISBN: 1-56523-255-0
Pages 80
8.5" x 11"

Fantasy & Legend Scroll Saw Puzzles
by Judy and Dave Peterson
Price: $14.95
Soft Cover
ISBN: 1-56523-256-9
Pages 80
8.5" x 11"

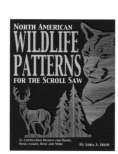

North American Wildlife Patterns for the Scroll Saw
61 Captivating Designs for Moose, Bear, Eagles, Deer and More
by Lora S. Irish
Price: $12.95
Soft Cover
ISBN: 1-56523-165-1
Pages 72
8.5" x 11"

Artistic Wildlife Projects for the Scroll Saw
Bears, Wild Cats, Bird of Prey and Other Predators from Around the World
by Marilyn Carmin
Price: $19.95
Soft Cover
ISBN: 1-56523-224-0
Pages 120
8.5" x 11"

LOOK FOR THESE BOOKS AT YOUR LOCAL BOOK STORE OR WOODWORKING RETAILER

Or call 800-457-9112 • Visit www.FoxChapelPublishing.com

Learn from the Experts

Fox Chapel Publishing is not only your leading resource for woodworking books, but also the publisher of the two leading how-to magazines for woodcarvers and woodcrafters!

WOOD CARVING ILLUSTRATED is the leading how-to magazine for woodcarvers of all skill levels and styles—providing inspiration and instruction from some of the world's leading carvers and teachers. A wide range of step-by-step projects are presented in an easy-to-follow format, with great photography and useful tips and techniques. *Wood Carving Illustrated* delivers quality editorial on the most popular carving styles, such as realistic and stylized wildlife carving, power carving, Santas, caricatures, chip carving and fine art carving. The magazine also includes tool reviews, painting and finishing features, profiles on carvers, photo galleries and more.

SCROLL SAW WORKSHOP is the leading how-to magazine for novice and professional woodcrafters. Shop-tested projects are complete with patterns and detailed instructions. The casual scroller appreciates the in-depth information that ensures success and yields results that are both useful and attractive; the pro will be creatively inspired with fresh and innovative design ideas. Each issue of *Scroll Saw Workshop* contains useful news, hints and tips, and includes lively features and departments that bring the world of scrolling to the reader.

Want to learn more about a subscription? Visit **www.FoxChapelPublishing.com** and click on either the *Wood Carving Illustrated* button or *Scroll Saw Workshop* button at the top of the page. Watch for our special **FREE ISSUE** offer! You can also write to us at 1970 Broad Street, East Petersburg, PA 17520 or call toll-free at 1-800-457-9112.